Herodotus: A Very Short Introduction

VERY SHORT INTRODUCTIONS are for anyone wanting a stimulating
and accessible way into a new subject. They are written by experts, and
have been translated into more than 45 different languages.

The series began in 1995, and now covers a wide variety of topics in
every discipline. The VSI library now contains over 500 volumes—a Very
Short Introduction to everything from Psychology and Philosophy of
Science to American History and Relativity—and continues to grow in every
subject area.

Titles in the series include the following:

Jennifer T. Roberts

HERODOTUS

A Very Short Introduction

OXFORD
UNIVERSITY PRESS

OXFORD

UNIVERSITY PRESS

Great Clarendon Street, Oxford ox2 6DP

Oxford University Press is a department of the University of Oxford.
It furthers the University's objective of excellence in research, scholarship,
and education by publishing worldwide in

Oxford New York

Auckland Cape Town Dar es Salaam Hong Kong Karachi
Kuala Lumpur Madrid Melbourne Mexico City Nairobi
New Delhi Shanghai Taipei Toronto

With offices in

Argentina Austria Brazil Chile Czech Republic France Greece
Guatemala Hungary Italy Japan Poland Portugal Singapore
South Korea Switzerland Thailand Turkey Ukraine Vietnam

Oxford is a registered trade mark of Oxford University Press
in the UK and in certain other countries

Published in the United States
by Oxford University Press Inc., New York

British Library Cataloguing in Publication Data
Data available

Library of Congress Cataloging in Publication Data
Data available

Typeset by SPI Publisher Services, Pondicherry, India
Printed and bound by
CPI Group (UK) Ltd, Croydon, CR0 4YY

ISBN: 978–0–19–957599–2

For Chris

Contents

List of illustrations

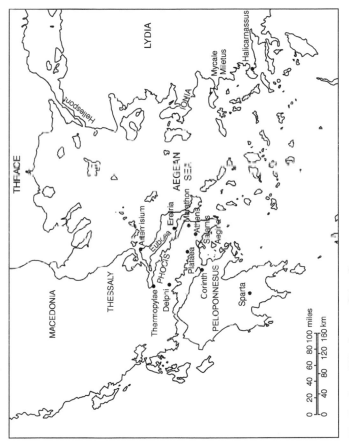

The Greek world in the age of Herodotus

Introduction

Ambrose Bierce was in good company when he dismissed history as an account of events brought about 'by rulers, mostly knaves, and soldiers, mostly fools'. Consider the words of the great historian of ancient Rome, Edward Gibbon, who labelled history 'little more than the register of the crimes, follies, and misfortunes of mankind'. Jane Austen added the absence of women into the mix, famously observing that history was all wars and plagues, the quarrels of the mighty, 'the men all so good for nothing, and hardly any women at all'. Who could have invented this dreadful thing? And when, and where, and why?

History as we know it came into being in Greece in the second half of the 5th century BC, a time and place of extraordinary cultural and intellectual fertility. Accounts of events had been compiled earlier, but such previous texts as survive were always assembled with a distinct agenda, designed to glorify this or that king of Assyria, say, or to demonstrate the hand of Yahweh in human affairs. It was the extraordinary achievement of the great Greek historians of the 5th century to take a page from the natural scientists and undertake research – *historia*, as it was called in their language – simply to expand their understanding of the past, the present, and perhaps the future, and to impart this understanding to a broad audience. Although the divine certainly showed its hand, *historia* was a largely secular project, designed to showcase human nature and its workings. Herodotus would surely have endorsed R. G. Collingwood's contention that the value of history 'is that it teaches us what man has done and thus what man is' – though he might have replaced 'man' with 'humanity' to make sure that women were included.

Two historians very different from one another busied themselves about this extraordinary enterprise, probably a generation apart. It was said that Herodotus, born around 484 BC, moved the young Thucydides to tears by reciting parts of his work. To the groundbreaking Herodotus, then, the Roman man of letters Cicero gave the title *pater historiae*, 'Father of History' – although he conceded that *The Histories* contained countless legends. (He was right about those legends, and we will be returning to them.) Herodotus's notion of *historia*, however, was not the 'maps and chaps' version that thinkers such as Bierce, Gibbon, and Austen professed to disdain. Although Herodotus was indubitably fascinated by both maps and chaps, there was a great deal more to his work than that.

For it was Herodotus who first undertook the daunting task of sorting myth from fact – Herodotus, indeed, who first saw a distinction between the two. Using inquiry, 'autopsy' (nothing to do with death – it is the Greek word for 'seeing for oneself'), oral tradition, and the brains he was born with, he produced a rich tapestry of a text organized around the central question of his youth: how did the Greeks and Persians come to war with each other, and what accounted for the Greek victory when the Persians so conspicuously had the advantage in both men and money? Herodotus spoke in his own voice as a private citizen. No king, no god gave him an imprimatur. And unlike his predecessor in the telling of very long stories, the author (or authors) of the *Iliad* and the *Odyssey*, he appealed to no muse; he was completely dependent upon his human sources – and his human powers of analysis. He was on his own.

Of course, it would be stretching the truth to claim that Herodotus boldly went where none had gone before. Some mini-histories had been composed, usually dealing with local traditions. Surviving fragments make clear that ethnography formed part of the prose *Journey around the World* composed by Hecataeus of Miletus around 500 BC. But nothing on the scale of Herodotus's *opus* had ever been undertaken. It was longer than either Homeric poem by far, and its scope was immense with respect to both time and space. Its principle of organization hung on the advance of the Persian juggernaut: each nation with which the Persians came into contact prior to their attack on Greece early in the 5th century received ethnographic treatment at greater or lesser length depending on the extent of Herodotus's information or the perceived interest of his Greek audience.

Our roving reporter, a thinker and traveller of insatiable curiosity, catches us up in his narrative by the intensity of his contagious thirst for knowledge. Whether about the true story of the abduction of Helen (she was never, Herodotus says, in Troy, but remained in Egypt throughout the war), the way the Scythians buried their kings (with many retainers), how the Trausians greet the birth of a baby (mourning the sufferings it will have to endure), how the Greeks and Persians came to blows (a very long story indeed), *Herodotus wants to know*. He would have heartily agreed with Polish journalist Ryszard Kapuściński (who travelled all over the world with a copy of *The Histories*) that 'Without trying to enter other ways of looking, perceiving, describing, we won't understand anything of the world.' And he imparts this burning desire to us as we read, for he not only wants to know about the broad diversity of customs and values in the world; he wants us to know too. A conspicuous lack of Greek chauvinism undergirded Herodotus's ethnography and spurred it on. Yet for all his tolerance, for all his praise of individual Persian customs – he greatly approves their practice of keeping a boy from his father for the first five years of his life, lest it be too upsetting to him if the child should die – he nowhere suggests that Eastern autocracy is as viable an institution as the variety of more broadly based governments that marked the Greek world.

'At the heart of good history', journalist Stephen Schiff once observed, 'is a naughty little secret: good storytelling'. Herodotus intrigues in part because he was a master storyteller. His long narrative, what the Greeks might have called a *logos*, a tale, consists of many shorter *logoi* stitched together, some just a few hundred words, some thousands, not always in strictly chronological order, ebbing and flowing and circling back around like a river whose course perpetually mystifies and delights. Herodotus's text is a demanding one. The *logoi* represent very different genres, ranging from forays into the political history of Athens and Sparta to whimsical anecdotes clearly grounded in folk motifs or fairy tales. Some have profound significance in the context of Herodotus's project; others do not. Nor is the pace consistent. Divided by some later scholar into nine 'books', the text moseys through centuries of history for several books – several hundred modern pages – and then assumes a much narrower focus as Herodotus moves us into the war years leading up to Xerxes' defeat.

What are we to make of a long, complex work cobbled together from oral sources of varying reliability by a man who loved to tell stories? Can we be sure that Herodotus went to all the places he says he did? Sober modern critics often seek to distance themselves from Herodotus, even at times going so far as to deny him the name of historian. In with maps and chaps, he has thrown hares, cannibals, mummies, pigs, dreams, prostitution, gold-digging ants, clever queens, bees, women who were gang-raped until they died, people who cannot so much as look at a bean, and a fart.

And worse still: *religion is pervasive* in *The Histories*. Though Herodotus portrays the course of the war as largely driven by human agents with human motivations and personalities, his text is peppered with oracles, prophecies, and outright declarations of belief. Where are we to locate a 'historical' work that includes some sense of divine presence in every major battle?

Fortunately, as fate would have it, while Herodotus weaves his tale(s), he creates space not only for the gods but for us, for you and for me, his audience. His constant intrusions of himself into the text keep constantly before our eyes the fact that he is an ordinary person wrestling with unruly material, much as we are invited to do. Introducing interviews into the record, reporting (or denying) eyewitness observation, claiming (or disclaiming) authority – overall, he makes some five hundred evaluative remarks of one kind or another (I know, I believe, I doubt, I don't know, I cannot say, I conjecture, it seems likely/unlikely, I have heard but do not believe....). The richness and ambiguity of this beguiling text provide challenges for the reader that draw him or her in. As we read, we find ourselves engaged in a constant dialogue with what we are reading. Herodotus frequently offers us several different versions of a number of historical events, sometimes supporting one over the others, sometimes leaving us to choose.

A wise man like Herodotus, who sorrowed over the pervasiveness of war, would have understood the strictures of Bierce and Gibbon, though he would have had no way of knowing his successors would latch onto his notion of the war monograph as the template for history but reject his unselfconscious incorporation of women. All in all, he would have been happier with the dictum of Droysen that 'History is the "know thyself" of humanity – the self-consciousness of mankind'. This richer, broader brand of history is what appears in the work that some call *The Persian Wars*, others, more faithfully to the Greek, *The Histories*, that is, *The Researches*.

Chapter 1
The world of Herodotus

The astonishing outcome of the Greco-Persian Wars made a profound impression on those alive at the time. It is conceivable that Herodotus remembered his parents' getting word of the Greek victory over Xerxes at Salamis in 480; one of Xerxes' chief admirals, Artemisia, was queen of Herodotus's own home town of Halicarnassus on the Anatolian coast, today the fashionable Turkish port of Bodrum, and she had fought valiantly in that battle. Herodotus's fascination with powerful females may well correlate with his childhood experience of this daring woman who actually commanded warships. Our historian may have been as much as five years old at the time of the final face-off, fought the following spring in Anatolia itself. From that time on, the stunning victory of the 'greatest generation' of Greeks remained a lively topic of conversation in the Hellenic world. The younger soldiers were still available for interviews in Herodotus's adulthood. They were probably flattered to be asked about their war experiences and eager to talk. Men and women of a postwar generation normally experience the war vicariously through dinner-table and other conversation – parents, aunts and uncles, grandparents, various contacts from this older world. Herodotus was almost certainly himself a friend of the playwright Sophocles, who was chosen in adolescence for the civic duty of leading the choral chant in celebration of the Greek naval victory at Salamis. In 472, Aeschylus produced his play *The Persians* about that

1. Helen Carey as Atossa and Ted van Griethuysen as Darius in the Shakespeare Theatre Company's 2006 production of Aeschylus' *The Persians*, a new version by Ellen McLaughlin, directed by Ethan McSweeny

victory, and the man who paid to have the play's chorus trained was Pericles, who would become the most prominent Athenian statesman of Herodotus's day. Throughout the Mediterranean world, the war lived on for generations as a defining moment in history. As the Athenian and Spartan alliances fought one another, first in an undeclared war lasting from 460 to 446, and then in the great Peloponnesian War of 431–404, memories of Greek unity lingered as a painful reminder of simpler times.

We know few details of Herodotus's life after his childhood in Halicarnassus. He probably was driven out in one of the episodes of civil strife so characteristic of Greek cities, spent much of his life travelling as an exile, visited Athens, and died on the opposite side of the Hellenic world in the Greek colony of Thurii in south Italy some time after 430, although some have placed his death at the northern fringe, in the Macedonian city of Pella. Late sources

7

report that his father was Lyxes, his mother Dryo or Rhoio or perhaps something else altogether. Of more importance is the name of another relative – an uncle, perhaps, or a cousin – the poet Panyassis, whom some readers praised (only after his death, alas) as second only to Homer; Panyassis wrote on the foundings of Greek cities in Ionia, as the west coast of Anatolia was known, placing Herodotus in a literary family, although he wrote in verse and thus provided only a partial precedent for Herodotus's remarkable undertaking.

The Halicarnassus of Herodotus's day stood at the crossroads of East and West, sporting a mixture of Greek and native inhabitants and cultures. The locals were Carians, some of whom Homer said fought as allies of Troy in the Trojan War. Our sketchy information about Herodotus's relatives includes both Greek names and Carian ones. Some readers, like Kapuściński, have ascribed the breadth of Herodotus's vision to this hybrid background, contending that 'half-breeds' who spend their youth amid different cultures, 'as a blend of different bloodlines, have their worldview determined by such concepts as border, distance, difference, diversity'. Herodotus's way of looking at things was no doubt shaped and enriched by the mixed culture of his native city, as well as by the perils of the imperial mindset that Athens had taken over from Persia.

The Greek cities of Ionia, moreover, were hotbeds of innovative and often audacious thought. In the absence of firmly established scientific methods, what we now think of as discrete intellectual disciplines – natural science, philosophy, psychology, theology – merged far more than they do today. Thales had speculated on the origins of matter and concluded that everything had originated as water. Anaximenes, on the other hand, believed that everything had evolved from air, which could become fire, wind, cloud, or (when condensed) solid, while Anaximander maintained that the first creatures arose from slime and that humans had evolved out of other animal species, and was the first Greek to draw a map of the known world. The long-lived Xenophanes, still around when Herodotus was born, conjectured that humans created gods rather than the other way around: if cattle and horses and lions could draw, he claimed irreverently, each animal would create images of gods in the likeness of its own species. Heraclitus, the man we associate with the claim that one can never step in the same river twice, maintained that everything was in flux. To this tradition of Ionian curiosity and scepticism Herodotus was heir.

At the same time, speculation was rife about the connections between geography and society. Herodotus's work was disseminated in speech and in writing before the famous physician Hippocrates reached the peak of his career, but Hippocrates' father and grandfather had been physicians, and the search for scientific explanations for disease that disavowed divine causes had been in progress for quite some time. The island of Cos where Hippocrates worked was just across the strait from Halicarnassus. Eyewitness observation, interview, evaluation of evidence, the use of analogy, and a cumulative analysis of data linked Herodotus's work to the world of the physicians. He no doubt learned from them, and they from him. All this goes a long way to explain the fertility of Herodotus's mind, his commitment to research, his intrepid curiosity about climate and topography, his openness to new ideas and tolerance of cultural diversity, but only an extraordinary drive could account for his decision to undertake an unprecedented work of this scope. Ranging widely in time and space, *The Histories* was too long to have been recited at a festival in its entirety. Even a tag team of readers would have required at least fifty hours for such a performance.

It is difficult for us today to grasp the novelty of a full-length book written in prose. We learn to speak and write in prose before we take on poetry. Some of us encounter metre only in singing, listening to music, or hearing nursery rhymes. Prose simply, well, *is*. Its omnipresence makes it invisible. It is the medium of newspapers, thrillers, instruction manuals, e-mail. This hierarchy was in many ways inverted in early Greece, where literature was composed first in verse and only later in prose. The Greeks of Herodotus's day, in fact, had no word for prose. Only a century or so later did the expression *psilos logos* come into use to categorize it ('naked speech', that is, speech unadorned by metre), or *pezos logos* ('language that goes on foot', unassisted by the winged chariot of poetry). The foundational texts of Greek civilization, the *Iliad* and the *Odyssey*, had been composed in verse. To them, one generation after another of Greeks turned for inspiring models of heroism, for lofty turns of expression, for an entire worldview – and for the notion of a rich, long narrative tale with many twists and turns. They were standard fare for recitation as after-supper entertainment in an age without electric lights, television, or the Internet.

Poetry was also the medium in which lyric poets like Sappho, from the island of Lesbos, complained of the pangs of love, in which the Athenian lawgiver Solon wrote of justice and politics, in which the exile Theognis wrote bitterly about the civil strife in his home state of Megara. Poets were often centrally involved in the lives of their cities, as they were considered teachers as well as artists and revered accordingly: compare our own day, in which many people would be hard put to name a living poet (or, in some cases, a dead one). It should come as no surprise that we know of several historical accounts of narrowly limited scope that were written in verse. Semonides from the island of Amorgos composed the *Early History of the Samians* around 650; it probably dealt with the foundation of Samos and may have been around 4,000 verses long (about a quarter as long as the *Iliad*, a third as long as the *Odyssey*). Some time later, Xenophanes composed the *Foundation of Colophon and Colonization of Elea*, about 2,000 lines in length. Shortly after the Persian Wars, Simonides of Ceos wrote longish poems on the topic and heroized the fallen at Plataea in Homeric style. Most conspicuously, Herodotus's relative Panyassis of Halicarnassus seems to have written about the foundation of the Greek colonies in Ionia in his *Ionika* of some 7,000 lines. Poetry formed the core of Greek education. The education of Greek boys – and the occasional girl – was remarkable both for what it taught and for what it didn't. A bit of maths was offered, but no social studies, no science. The essence of Greek education was *mousike*, poetry set to the music of the lyre. *Mousike* took its name from the goddesses who inspired it, the Muses, and gave us in turn the word 'music'; from the lyre, we get 'lyrics'. Though Herodotus cited any number of poets in his *Histories*, it was primarily Homer's majestic work that infused his own and offered both harmony and counterpoint to his narrative. (By 'Homer' is meant the guiding intelligence that informed the poems we know today as the *Iliad* and the *Odyssey*; this is hardly the place to speculate as to whether the author was one person, two different people, or a committee of dozens.) For Homer had provided the template for both the war story and the travel tale rife with wonders.

Prose writing, of course, was not unheard of in Herodotus's day. Anaximander and Anaximenes both seem to have used prose to convey their ideas. Heraclitus deposited a work of philosophy in prose in the magnificent temple of Artemis at Ephesus, one of the Seven Wonders of the Ancient World (the temple, that is, not the book). Around the end of the 6th century, Greeks began to write down the great legends of the past in prose, becoming what we call 'mythographers'. Tying together these myths were elaborate genealogies of gods and heroes, and by the beginning of the 5th century, a number of such genealogies were in circulation. The most prominent among these was that of Hecataeus, who probably died around the year of Herodotus's birth; he traced the lineage of prominent Greek families back to divine ancestors in his *Genealogies* and used rational analysis to tone down some of the more outlandish myths he encountered (but not to discard them out of hand). Hecataeus also used prose to compose his *Journey around the World*. He plainly partook of the scepticism that was sweeping Ionia and in which Herodotus certainly shared. One surviving fragment proclaims: 'Hecataeus of Miletus says the following: I write what I consider true, for the stories of the

Greeks are many and appear to me ridiculous.' Herodotus mentions Hecataeus on more than one occasion and seems to have relied on him from time to time.

In Herodotus's own day, prose came into its own, particularly in the burgeoning democracy of Athens, where the first laws had been written in prose already in the late 7th century, and skill in public speaking – in the assemblies, in the courts – was soon on a par with birth, wealth, and military prowess. The itinerant philosopher/rhetoricians known as sophists were eagerly at hand to instruct young men in this increasingly valued art of persuasion. Because of their propensity for looking at old questions from new angles (and questioning what had never been questioned before, at least out loud), their detractors accused them of making a living by teaching uppity adolescents to disrespect gods and parents. But in fact, what they did was in many ways no different from what teachers – the good ones – do today: teach youth to question authority and make solid arguments. And it was not only in Athens that they plied their wares. Though by no means all Greek cities developed democracies, the spirit of open debate and rebuttal characteristic of the 5th century dovetailed nicely with the flourishing outburst of intellectual speculation that had marked the 6th to lay the groundwork for the kind of analytical inquiry found in Herodotus's work.

Ultimately, *The Histories* was a profoundly democratic text, with its multi-subjectivity, its open invitation to readers to make up their own minds and stand always in the position of evaluators. And not only that: the very existence of democratic (or at least non-monarchic) forms of government had created a universe where history could be made by ordinary people – by the same people who might read, or listen to, Herodotus's work. Poetry had been the language of the gods; prose was the language of people, a medium in which they could challenge other people and even the gods themselves. It is quite possibly this multi-subjectivity that accounts for the recent rise in popularity of Herodotus. Once considered frivolous when placed side by side with the didactic and relentlessly serious Thucydides, *The Histories* has now come to be appreciated for its openness to competing views, its cultural relativity, its interest in social history, and its acknowledgement of the existence of two sexes. (Of course, not everyone's reaction is as drastic as that of Egyptology professor Salima Ikram, who rolled her eyes at the notion of placing Thucydides above Herodotus and cried out 'Okay, so Thucydides is a finer historian, but he's so dull, so tedious, oh my God, I'm going to shoot myself!')

While it was the existence of verse that had facilitated the creation of the Homeric epics, works that could be memorized and sung to a spellbound audience, it was prose served up with a dollop of genius that made possible the creation of history – the opening up of a whole complex of relationships between an investigator and his/her informants, finished text, and audience. For the give and take of argumentation that we find in the sophists, the wrangling of the Athenian assembly and the law courts, provided fertile ground for the analysis of an incalculable mass of theory and fact in the context of the broadest of human concerns. Even after we have patiently heard out all the caveats about Herodotus's lapses in judgement, exaggerated numbers, and dependence on unreliable informants; even after we have been hit over the head again and again with claims of the more 'scientific' nature of Thucydides' work; even after we have listened to allegations that Herodotus did not travel as widely as he claimed or see all the things he claimed to have seen at first hand; we are left with the fact that Herodotus unmistakably invented the writing of history: one day it was not there, and then suddenly it was.

Well, perhaps not so suddenly, as *The Histories* took decades to compose, but, say, within a generation. Earlier writers had analysed the workings of the universe, had written up their travels, had explored the meaning of myths, had composed accounts of local happenings in a corner of the world. But they had not endowed their work with a *focus* or imbued it with forward drive. Their writings, little of which survive, no doubt contained many stories – but not stories that added up to a really big story larger than the sum of its parts, one that culminated in a climax that would affect the life of every listener and reader Herodotus could have anticipated, and in fact has affected our lives down to this century. For without the miraculous defeat of Persia by a small band of Greek states fighting to stave off slavery, there would have been no Parthenon, no *Oedipus Rex*, no Socrates, no Plato, no Aristotle. Without the Greek victory, it is difficult to imagine the history of Western philosophy – or of Western political thought, grounded as it is in the irony that the Athenians both created democracy and gave birth to the very men who established the anti-democratic tradition in political thinking.

Herodotus could not have foreseen the entire course of Western philosophy and political theory, but he knew the difference between totalitarianism and freedom, and he saw in the defeat of the first by the second a grand theme. Grand, but not an unadulterated triumph where the Greeks were concerned. For just as the Persian Wars 'made' Herodotus, they also 'made' Athens – into a glittering cultural hub that its foremost statesman Pericles would describe, in the pages of Thucydides, as 'the school of Greece', but also into an increasingly greedy and power-hungry imperial state that evoked the Persian Empire in the worst way. Just as the *Iliad* ended with Achilles yet to die but certain to do so, the cloud of Athenian imperialism hangs over Herodotus's carefully crafted narrative and gives it much of its poignancy, as its author surely intended.

Herodotus lived not only on the boundary between the Greek-speaking city states of the Eastern Mediterranean and the Persian Empire in Anatolia and at the dawn of prose but in another liminal zone as well: he lived at a time when a literate mindset was beginning to contend with an oral one among the educated classes. This is not to say that Greeks who had gone to school before the 5th century could not read, but they may not have used reading a great deal in their lives, and through much of the 5th century, listening remained for many the customary way of absorbing language, whether on the stage, where tragedies were invariably written in verse, or declamations in court, a prose medium. It has been said with some justice that Herodotus came at the end of a long oral tradition and his younger contemporary Thucydides at the beginning of a literate one – Thucydides, who, in a slap at Herodotus, carped that his own work was composed not for applause after a splashy recitation but as a possession for all time. Herodotus, we might say, transcribed speech, whereas Thucydides inscribed thought. It is this difference that explains the contrast between Herodotus's delightfully relaxed narrative, composed in what Aristotle called the 'strung-along style', one unit flowing naturally into another, and the sinewy prose of Thucydides, whose tight, sometimes contorted, syntax has been the despair of many a Greek student throughout the ages.

Heard or read, the text of the historian raises an inevitable question: how can we trust what this person says/writes? In poetry, there was no question of the creator's authority. The poet offered only one version of events, and, despite the insertion of speeches into his or her work, spoke in effect with one voice. Often that was the voice of the Muse. Both *Iliad* and *Odyssey* had begun with an appeal to the Muse. 'Sing, goddess, the wrath of Achilles, son of Peleus...' begins the *Iliad*; the *Odyssey* opens with 'Sing to me, Muse, of the man of many devices....' Later on, it might be the voice of the poet herself, as Sappho proclaims, for example, that no sight is as beautiful as that of the beloved. Nobody is going to question them. No sceptic will say, 'Can you prove that? What's your evidence?' Historians, however, who can present the contested voices of their many sources as they wrangle with them to mould a coherent picture of the past, must justify their claims to knowledge and understanding. History offers both challenge and opportunity. The historian's sources must be gathered before they can be assembled and integrated. To gather them, the historian may read books (of which there were few to hand in Herodotus's day), examine official records (not too many of those around either), interview informants, scrutinize material evidence, and, in many cases, travel. Once gathered, the data must be wrestled into shape in a manner that spurs the reader (or listener) to engage with the text – but to do so without discounting the authority of the historian, without dismissing the museless artist's claims to know. Again and again, realizing that he cannot be believed implicitly like a poet, Herodotus will have to persuade us – by argument, by analogy, by the citation of eyewitness evidence or the words of oral informants – that he knows what he is talking about as he writes in this protean genre we call history.

We would dearly love to know how Herodotus wrote this sprawling work. Did he make notes as he went along? Did he dictate to a slave who accompanied him on his travels? Writing in Greece was a difficult matter, revising even more so. Books were actually long scrolls of papyrus, an expensive and unwieldy material that discouraged the writing (or purchasing) of long works. Herodotus's *Histories* probably accounted for thirty such rolls. Revision presented substantial logistical obstacles, yet Herodotus frequently seems to comment on reactions to his work, remarking, for example, that some Greeks were not persuaded by his claim that prior to his accession Darius and two other Persians held a discussion about the comparative merits of monarchy, oligarchy, and democracy – but this conversation, he insists, really did take place. Such asides suggest that he gave trial readings of selected passages on various occasions and had some sense of how controversial statements were coming across. The notion of a particular date of 'publication' is not a meaningful concept in a world in which hardly anyone could afford to buy a book. Eventually, of course, the work was indeed published, probably not long before Herodotus's death, but portions, at least, surely had a vigorous life in oral presentation for some time before that.

2. As in the Nile delta, papyrus grows here in the Okavango delta in Botswana

The monumental obstacles Herodotus faced make his undertaking all the more astonishing, but he was not easily daunted. His first sentence outlines a formidable agenda:

> This is the setting forth of the research of Herodotus of Halicarnassus, put down here so that human accomplishments will not be blotted out with the passing of time, nor great and marvellous achievements – some displayed by Greeks, some by foreigners – lack renown; and, finally, to show why the two peoples fought with each other.

Herodotus's motivation, in other words, was twofold: to memorialize great accomplishments, and to demonstrate the causes of the Persian Wars. In his desire that great things not become *aklea*, renown-less, he echoes Homer writing about the aristocrats at Troy who fought for *kleos*, renown; when Odysseus leads an embassy to Achilles' tent in the *Iliad*, he finds Achilles holding the lyre and singing the *klea andron*, the glorious deeds of men. Herodotus's vision, however, was broader, for he sought to memorialize magnificent buildings, tombs, natural wonders, as well as actions, and much of what he sought to keep alive in memory was the work not of men, but in fact of women. Though his immediate successors showed no interest in women, in other respects his efforts met with success. For despite the many references that make clear his assumption of a Greek audience (such as 'I shall not describe the camel since Greeks already know what a camel looks like'), the breadth of his interests and sympathies, his sensitivity to the sorrows of the human condition, gave his work a long reach and has extended its appeal to readers in worlds of which even he, with his openness to the exotic, would never have dreamed. It is not only the enduring legend of Thermopylae, deployed in contexts from the liberation of Greece from Turkish domination to a French graveyard in Vietnam, that we owe to *The Histories*. Tales like those of the Amazons and the adventures of Cambyses in Egypt have fascinated archaeologists and explorers, novelists and anthropologists, throughout the ages.

Translated repeatedly from the Renaissance to the present, Herodotus's text engaged the English geographer James Rennell, who in addition to his work *The Geographical System of Herodotus* (1800) developed the first approximately correct map of India, as well as studies on the geography of northern Africa; it accompanied the explorer Lásló Almásy into the desert from the 1920s to his death in 1951 (the fictional Almásy served as the central character in Michael Ondaatje's novel *The English Patient*); Herodotus guided the Polish foreign correspondent Ryszard Kapuściński as his work took him through India, Sudan, the Congo, Cambodia, Afghanistan, Rangoon, and China; and inspired the British journalist Justin Marozzi to pack a suitcase and follow Herodotus's route, using the occasion to offer a meditation on the pointlessness of war (and to pass on, like Herodotus, what he heard from his interlocutors, such as Salima Ikram's facetious threat to shoot herself in contemplation of Thucydides' purported dullness). More than once in this book, the perspectives found in these 'continuators' of Herodotus comment on just what Herodotus was, and was not, doing in his *Histories*. Indeed, they are engaged in a dialogue not only with Herodotus but with one another; Kapuściński draws heavily on Ondaatje, and in Marozzi's book his friend Antigoni scolds Kapuściński for his take on the historian. Herodotus's message, she says, is:

> know the limits of the human condition. It's nothing to do with don't exploit other people, be nice to them, that's Kapuściński's Christian, humanist nonsense. Completely ridiculous. No, Herodotus is saying, don't think you'll be happy for ever and ever and don't place yourself above the gods.

These continuators will not, however, answer all the questions that have been raised about Herodotus's work. How accurate, for example, are Herodotus's amazing reports of the far-flung universe that was grist for his mill? To this question, we will return later on.

Chapter 2
Origins and the historian

A famous tale recounts the challenge posed to a distinguished lecturer by an indomitable woman in his audience. Dismissing his explication of the heliocentric system as hogwash, this elderly lady insisted that, rather, the Earth was a flat plate resting on the back of a tortoise. Inevitably (and not without a certain smugness), the lecturer asked just what his challenger thought the tortoise might be standing on. 'You're very clever, young man, very clever', his combative interlocutor replied. 'But it's turtles all the way down.' Some say the lecturer was Bertrand Russell, others William James, and still others say that nothing of the kind ever happened. A Hindu thinker is said to have provided an alternative version in which the world rested upon an elephant and the elephant rested upon a tortoise, and when questioned about the support system of the tortoise, he suggested…changing the subject. Herodotus, who loved collecting and comparing variants, would have been charmed.

The fame and diversity of these (apocryphal?) tales attest not only to the difficulty of accessing origins but also to the compelling human impulse to get at the beginnings of things – compelling to all reflective people, but of particular interest to historians. For without an understanding of origins, there can be no understanding of causality, and without causality…well, without the drive to understand causality, Herodotus would remain a geographer like Hecataeus, who reported on the customs he encountered in his wide travels; a poet like Simonides, who glorified Persian War heroes in Homeric fashion, or Pindar, whose celebratory odes incorporated mythical tales; or a storyteller like Aesop, who enchanted with his pointed animal fables. Without causality, the concept of history is meaningless. For all his interest in causality, however, Herodotus also understood how easy it was to go astray and wind up with a ridiculously simplistic model. He begins, in fact, by recounting entertaining myths about the distant origins of the cosmic war of East and West, only to brush them aside and move purposefully to the far more trustworthy realm of history.

Learned Persians, he says, place the blame for the hostility between Greeks and Persians on Phoenician traders, who while purveying their wares at Argos in mainland Greece snatched Io, the king's daughter. This abduction prompted some Greeks to carry off Europa from Tyre in Phoenicia and Medea from Colchis on the Black Sea. (A variant had Io running off of her own free will since she had gotten pregnant by the captain of the Phoenician ship.) The Trojan prince Paris in turn grabbed Helen from Sparta, thus triggering the Greek invasion of Troy. In the Persians' view, Herodotus reports, it was the capture of Troy that made them enemies of the Greeks, since 'the Persians consider Asia and the barbarian peoples living there as their domain, Europe and Greece being separate'. Well, Herodotus continues, having entertained us with these salacious tales, I have no way of knowing whether any of this is true:

> Rather, I prefer to stick to what I do know and to point out just who
> first did injury to the Greeks; then I will proceed with my story,
> giving detailed accounts of small cities as well as great ones. After
> all, many that were great in the past have since become small, and
> many that were great in my own time were small in earlier times.
> Knowing, therefore, that human prosperity never remains long in
> the same place, I will discuss both alike.

(Commenting on this line, Ondaatje's fictional Almásy observes that he and his fellow geographers, traversing the desert with a copy of *The Histories*, 'knew great power and great finance were temporary things. We all slept with Herodotus.') The limits of human knowledge; the concern with firsts; the identification of himself as the author of a text; the mutability of fortune: all these key elements in *The Histories* emerge from this short passage.

Who, then, was it, who first did injury to the Greeks? What was the lowest rung on the ladder of causality that led to the Persian Wars? Croesus, the ruler of Lydia, Herodotus says, was the first foreigner of whom we know to have come into contact with the Greeks, levying tribute on some and making alliances with others. This will soon prove important, since when Cyrus and his Medes conquer Croesus and the Lydians, the tribute-paying Greek cities will find themselves under a more exacting master.

The phrase 'the first of whom we know' appears with remarkable frequency in *The Histories*, signalling both Herodotus's fascination with firsts and his awareness of the limited scope of human knowledge. Polycrates of Samos, Herodotus reports,

> was the first Greek of whom we know to plan the dominion of the sea – unless we count Minos of Cnossus or any other who may possibly have ruled the sea at an earlier date. In ordinary human history at any rate, Polycrates was the first.

Gyges was the first foreigner of whom we know, after Midas, the king of Phrygia, to make offerings at Delphi. The Lydians were the first of whom we know to strike and use coins of gold and silver. Arion, so far as we know, was the first to compose and name the verse form known as the dithyramb. The excursus on Egypt that forms Book 2 is rife with firsts, since it was in large part Egypt's very antiquity that had captured Herodotus's imagination. The Egyptians, Herodotus says, were the first to use the names of the twelve gods that the Greeks later took over, the first to tell a man's fortune by his birthday, and the first to originate ceremonial meetings and processions and teach them to the Greeks. The pharaoh Psammetichus even undertook a Herodotean experiment to determine whether the Egyptians were indeed, as they had thought, the oldest race in the world. Sequestering two newborns with no company but a shepherd and his flocks, he waited for the shepherd to report what the first word was that the children spoke. When they began to exclaim '*bekos*' while running to him with outstretched hands, the shepherd reported this to Psammetichus. Upon inquiry, the pharaoh learned that this was the Phrygian word for bread. Overlooking the possibility that the children were simply mimicking the bleating of their lamby companions, the Egyptians conceded that the Phrygians were the oldest race in the world and they themselves were the second oldest. (They were, of course, unaware of the subsequent experiment of King James V of Scotland that demonstrated that toddlers left to their own devices will speak Hebrew.)

Enough with Egyptian and Phrygian firsts. How did Croesus, 'the first of whom we know' to have come into contact with the Greeks, get to be king of Lydia?

Croesus, it seems, owed his position to his great-great-grandfather Gyges. And that is where Herodotus will really begin his story, because the story of Gyges is just too meaty to leave out. It offers Herodotus an opportunity to draw on his full powers of dramatization; it illustrates several of his central themes; and it leads him into the story of Croesus, which in turn feeds into the career of Cyrus and the establishment of the Persian Empire, without which there would be no Persian Wars. We see here a persistent characteristic of Herodotus's style, a sort of backstitch in which a declarative statement is immediately amended by a second thought that reconfigures the narrative: I will begin with Croesus, he says . . . but, no, I think we should start with Gyges.

The Lydian king Candaules, we learn, was fated to end badly. Being so fated, and having mysteriously conceived a passion for his own wife (of all people!), Candaules made a habit of going on and on to a favourite bodyguard about her beauty. (By now, Herodotus is in full dramatic mode.) Convinced that his bodyguard – to wit, Croesus's ancestor, Gyges – is insufficiently persuaded of the queen's pulchritude, Candaules proposes that he behold her naked. After all, he argues, people are accustomed to place more trust in eyes than ears. (This is also a commentary on Herodotus's methods of historical research, in which he gives priority to 'aut-opsy', eyewitness evidence.) Gyges cries out in horror: Master! This is outlandish! I absolutely believe everything you say about your wife's beauty, and I beg you not to make me do this thing that is so contrary to custom.

Candaules will not be moved. Forced to observe the queen as she undresses for bed, Gyges is caught, and the dishonoured queen gives him the choice of facing execution or assassinating Candaules and ruling the kingdom with her. As Herodotus says in a short, pointed sentence, 'He chose to live'. After the murder of the king, Gyges was confirmed in his position by the oracle at Delphi, though the priestess there cautioned that vengeance would come for his actions in the fifth generation. As so often in *The Histories*, no attention was paid to this prophecy until it was realized. But realized it was, and the man who paid the penalty for Gyges' actions was none other than Croesus. The impulse to see Croesus as a forerunner of Xerxes and to see his life story as programmatic for *The Histories* as a whole is irresistible, but it is important to recognize that Herodotus's Croesus is in fact a liminal figure: Lydia was the westernmost of the eastern autocracies Herodotus discusses, and Croesus cared very much about the Greek world, seeking allies among the Greeks, and, like his ancestor Gyges, making offerings – very lavish ones, indeed – at Delphi.

Though the chronology of their meeting is dubious, tradition evidently left room for an encounter between Croesus and Solon, who was known to have travelled extensively in the 6th century after overhauling Athens' legal and economic system. Having seen to it that Solon is given the grand tour of his treasury, the Lydian king asks him whom he considers the most fortunate of men. Croesus has made the mistake of asking a question to which he does not really want to hear the answer: all he wants is for Solon to tell him that it is he, Croesus of Lydia, who is by far the most fortunate. Such a response, of course, would be both artistically anti-climactic and philosophically un-Greek. Solon instead names an Athenian of solid but not aristocratic stock – Tellos, a citizen of sufficient means 'by our standards' (translation: wealth of Eastern potentates not necessary for happiness) who had fine children and grandchildren and died fighting in defence of the city, honoured by all. Predictably, Croesus is underwhelmed by this cautionary tale and asks pointedly who might be the second happiest person Solon has seen.

No sale. Solon names two young men of Argos who yoked themselves to the family ox-cart and dragged their mother nearly six miles to the temple of Hera for the goddess's festival when the oxen were late returning from the fields. In answer to their mother's prayer, the youths received the greatest blessing available to mortals: they fell asleep in the temple (no doubt quite exhausted) and never awoke.

Croesus's complete failure to grasp Solon's message leads the Athenian to spell it out for him. Croesus, he says, humans are entirely creatures of chance. I cannot tell you if you are fortunate until I know that you have died happily, for 'Often enough god gives a man a glimpse of happiness only to ruin him utterly in the end'. Croesus dismisses Solon as an ignoramus, but Nemesis soon overtakes the Lydian king. Because his vainglorious self-satisfaction has provoked divine anger, he loses his beloved son Atys in a boar hunt, accidentally slain by, of all people, a suppliant whom Croesus had generously taken to his hearth. (Croesus can be a little oblivious, but he is not altogether a bad guy.) For two years afterwards, he grieved until disturbing news from the East pulled him out of the doldrums. The energetic Cyrus, it seemed, was transforming Persia into a power to be reckoned with. This development moved Croesus to seek advice from the oracles of Greece and Libya with an eye to a pre-emptive strike. (Like Herodotus, Croesus is something of a researcher.) The rest is history. Encouraged by the oracle at Delphi to think a great empire would fall if he attacked, he went to war with Cyrus. Of course, he had misunderstood the oracle. Given the proclivity of Herodotus's characters to misunderstand oracles at every possible turn, we could hardly expect anything else. The power Croesus destroyed was his own. Lydia was absorbed into the Persian Empire, and Croesus narrowly escaped death at Cyrus's hands.

Herodotus's narrative does not always move in a linear fashion. We do not hear of Cyrus's origins, for example, until quite some time after he and Croesus have come to blows. When we finally discover how Cyrus came to attain the stature that he did and to found the Persian Empire, we learn that plans were laid before Cyrus's birth to see to it that he never saw toddlerhood. A dream had frightened the Median monarch Astyages regarding his daughter's child: in sleep, he saw young Mandane urinating all over Asia, and he nervously married her to a Persian of middling status; later he dreamt of a vine growing out of her vagina to cover the same territory and decided to do away with the child she was carrying. But as is customary in these tales of the narrow escape of the future leader (Moses, Romulus, etc.), Cyrus had a lucky break. Astyages' henchman Harpagus, instructed to make away with the infant, in fact gives him to a herdsman to be killed, and the herdsman – for, of course, this is the lad that's born to be king – shares with his wife the upbringing of the royal babe.

When Cyrus, having learned his true identity, grows to manhood, he mobilizes the Persians to line up behind him and overthrow Astyages. Summoning men from the most powerful tribes, he orders them to clear a certain patch of rough and thorny land about eighteen or twenty furlongs square. This done, he slaughters huge numbers of goats, sheep, and oxen in preparation for a lavish banquet, adding fine wine and bread into the mix. When the Persians appear on the next day, he asks them which they prefer, the labours of the previous day or the delights of the current one. Hearing the predictable answer, Cyrus promises that if they rebel from Astyages, they will be able to enjoy a thousand pleasures as fine as the banquet before them – but that if they decline, the miserable labour of the previous day will form the template of many wretched tasks to come. 'I am the man', he says, 'destined by providence to undertake your liberation. I believe that you are a match for the Medes in everything, warfare included. I speak the truth. Do not delay, but rise up against Astyages this very minute.' Thus Cyrus, who never forgot his origins and the injury that had nearly cost him his life as an infant, overthrows Astyages and rules for many years, conquering Lydia and a great deal of other territory. He is succeeded by his problematic son Cambyses, who in time is succeeded by Darius. And with Darius, the open confrontation between Greeks and Persians begins.

But who are these Greeks? What are *their* origins? Herodotus's engagement with this question – indeed, his very openness to engaging with it – reveals a different Herodotus from the storytelling Herodotus who has narrated the engaging tales of Gyges, of Croesus, of Cyrus. In a famous passage in Book 8, the Athenians assure the Spartans that they would never cut a deal with Persia, for to do so would betray *to Hellenikon* – 'Greekness': 'one race speaking a single language, with shrines and sacrifices in common, a similar way of life'. Not long afterwards, they threaten to make precisely such a deal, and in fact at different junctures Herodotus undermines the notion that the Greeks possessed a unique and unified culture.

All of Greece, he points out, was originally inhabited by the barbarian people called Pelasgians, of whom the Athenians of his day were direct descendants. He greeted with sarcasm the claim that the inhabitants of the twelve Ionian cities of Asia Minor were somehow of purer and nobler Ionian descent than others, since a good number of the original settlers came from non-Ionian cities – and indeed, from some that were not even Greek! He also stresses Phoenician influence: the revered Athenian heroes Harmodius and Aristogeiton, he says, belonged to a clan that was not, as they claimed, from Eretria, north of Athens, but in fact of Phoenician origin, as was, he maintains, the alphabet. Herodotus gives the Greeks no quarter in stressing the diverse sources of their borrowings: from the Lydians, most of their games, and from the Carians, helmet crests, shield emblems, and shield handles; from the Libyans, the outfit in which Athena was normally portrayed. The identities of all the gods, he maintained, were learned from non-Greeks, particularly the Egyptians; compared to the Egyptians, the Greeks had come to their knowledge of the gods 'only yesterday or the day before yesterday, so to speak'. I could supply a good deal of evidence, he says, in support of the idea that the Greeks got the name of Heracles from Egypt rather than the other way around. Normally – though not invariably – a cultural diffusionist, Herodotus ascribes the invention of altars, temples, statues, religious processions, and the doctrine of reincarnation to the Egyptians, and more often than not he maintains that the Greeks borrowed these institutions; in the case of reincarnation, in fact, he even accuses the Greek borrowers of outright theft. (Egyptologists report that he is wrong here, but his thinking contrasts strikingly with that of the more chauvinistic Hecataeus, who was convinced that the influence went the other way around.)

Both in his storytelling mode and in his ethnographic mode, then, Herodotus manifests a strong belief that to understand history one must understand origins. He is aware that national pride leads people to offer sanitized versions of their origins that downplay racial mixture and cultural borrowing. Throughout *The Histories*, he engages with the origins of origins, noting that the traditions about traditions are suspect, and that we must always consider the source. Those who censure Herodotus for some of the taller tales in his text should remember his role in the foundation of source criticism.

Chapter 3

Greeks and Persians at war

Nowhere does Herodotus draw more successfully on his skills as a dramatist than in his treatment of the bloody Persian Wars themselves. The centrepiece of *The Histories*, the wars between Greece and Persia do not explode onto the stage until over halfway through the narrative, but when they do, they rush in a torrent to their conclusion. They are sped along by Herodotus's strong convictions about human nature in all its variety: the consuming thirst for revenge; the propensity of Eastern potentates to desire ever more possessions; the tragic consequences of not heeding wise advisers telling truth to power; the perils of absolutism; the fawning of royal toadies with their own agendas; the do-or-die heroism of the stolid Greek infantryman; the energies unleashed by democracy. The tension is constant between the knowledge of the outcome and the very improbability of that result. Of course, victory would go to the Greeks; the Greeks did win, the audience knows, and both omens and humans warned the proud Xerxes of troubles ahead.

On the other hand, how, really, could what happened actually have occurred? How could a band of thirty-odd small states accustomed to constant bickering with one another, not to mention endless internal squabbling, possibly defeat the largest empire the world had ever seen? Herodotus's interpretation of

3. Xerxes here appears in his youth as crown prince of Persia, standing behind his father Darius among the abundant relief sculptures in the treasury at the Persian capital of Persepolis

the Greek victory as simultaneously incredible and inevitable – the defeat of the Persian Goliath by the Greek David – shapes his narrative and heightens the excitement of his audience. The triumphal motif of this symphony resounds *fortissimo* in a major key, sweeping along with vigour as it swells and surges to its breathless finale. We are dealing with a work of art here, not dry annals; consequently, there are elements of dramatic reconstruction and exaggeration. You or I might write up the wars differently. But let us listen to the story as Herodotus tells it, suspending disbelief long enough to take it in, despite our suspicions that all could not have happened *precisely* as he says.

Oppressed by increased taxes and urged on by self-interested leaders, the Ionian Greeks rebel from the Persian Empire. Aristagoras of Miletus materializes in Sparta seeking aid from King Cleomenes. (Sparta, unlike other Greek states, retained the system of monarchy, though kings from two royal families reigned concurrently.) He is foiled by Cleomenes' spunky daughter Gorgo, aged 8 or 9, who cautions her father against Aristagoras's attempts at bribery, crying out 'Father, you had better get up and leave or your visitor will corrupt you'. The Athenians were more receptive, agreeing to supply 20 ships to the rebellion and prompting Herodotus's observation that it seems to be easier to fool a crowd than an individual. The rebellion is a failure, and in the course of it, Croesus's old capital Sardis catches fire. Upon hearing that the Athenians were involved, Darius asks who these people are, and on hearing the answer:

> He is said to have asked for his bow; he took hold of it, put an arrow on the string, and shot it up towards the sky. And as he fired it into the air, he said, 'Oh Zeus, grant that I may punish the Athenians'. Then he commanded one of his attendants to repeat to him three times, whenever he sat down to dinner, 'Master, remember the Athenians'.

4. Whatever the historicity of Herodotus's tale of Darius and the arrow, the Persians were certainly known as great archers. The archer king depicted with bow and arrow on this 5th-century Persian coin known as a daric (after Darius) may be Xerxes. The Athenians, on the other hand, marked their coins with the owl, the symbol of their wise patron goddess. This silver coin was a popular one, the tetradrachm (four drachma coin)

Darius did remember the Athenians, and the upshot was the battle fought on the plain of Marathon. The Athenians were understandably apprehensive about engaging the king's large army, but one of their generals, Miltiades, delivered a stirring speech that won the day: the generals had been divided about whether to fight or withdraw, but a democratic vote among them decided the matter. The fighting resulted in a stunning victory for the Athenian hoplite force. Herodotus does not tell us what a hoplite is; he assumed that his Greek audience would have been intimately familiar with the round shield (*hoplon*), spear, thrusting dagger, and helmet that were standard gear, accompanied in some cases by the protection of greaves. It would have struck a Greek as quite a feat for the Athenians to charge the Persians, as Herodotus claims, at a run, for the distance between the two forces was about a mile, and hoplite weaponry might weigh in at 35 pounds or more. The struggle was long and drawn out. The Persian centre broke the Greek line, but the Athenians on one wing and their allies the Plataeans on the other were victorious and, drawing into a single unit, fell on the Persians who had broken through in the centre and cut them down as they headed for the sea. A total of 192 Athenians died – Herodotus gives no number for the Plataean dead – but Persian losses were far higher: 6,400. After the battle, the Persian fleet headed for Athens, but realizing that the Athenians had gotten there first, it turned around and sailed back to Asia.

Incensed, Darius resolves on a second invasion: the Athenians now will have to pay for not only Sardis but Marathon as well. While he is raising troops and commissioning provisions, however, he dies. The Greek war falls to his son and successor Xerxes. Egged on by the shameless flattery of his ambitious cousin Mardonius, who aspires to govern a new province of Greece, Xerxes disregards the wise counsel of his uncle Artabanus, who makes an eminently Greek argument in favour of moderating imperial desires. You see, says Artabanus,

> how the god blasts with his thunderbolt creatures of more than
> common greatness and does not allow them to display their
> superiority, while small creatures don't annoy him at all; you can
> see that it's always on the largest buildings and the tallest trees that
> his bolts fall; for it is heaven's way to curb excess.

The king is unmoved, and he allows himself to be drawn into the project of punishing the Athenians. Xerxes, it proves, loves punishing. Indeed, he resolves to punish Artabanus himself for advising against the invasion of Greece and snickers that he will be assigned to remain at home with the women while he and the real men are off punishing the Athenians. And not only that. When the wealthy Lydian Pythius had offered to put all his money at Xerxes' disposal, the king had made the splashy gesture of rewarding him by instead making a donation to his estate that would bring his fortune up to a round number. Now, however, when Pythius asks Xerxes to allow just one of his five sons to stay home to look after

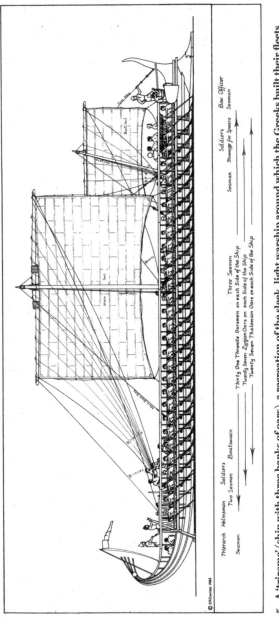

5. A 'trireme' (ship with three banks of oars), a recreation of the sleek, light warship around which the Greeks built their fleets

him in his old age while the others accompany the expedition to Greece, the fuming king orders his men to find Pythius's oldest son and cut him in half. The army was then instructed to march between the two halves of the young man's body.

Xerxes' punishments extend to inanimate objects. When the bridge he had built across the Hellespont is destroyed by a violent storm, the king orders his men to give the water 300 lashes and speak 'arrogant words that you would never hear from a Greek':

> 'You bitter water, this is your punishment for wronging your master when he did no wrong to you. King Xerxes will cross you, whether you permit it or not. People are right not to sacrifice to muddy, brackish waters like you!'

He also had those who had been in charge of building the bridge beheaded. He has separated what nature intended to be one – the two halves of Pythius's son's body – and joined what nature had made separate – Asia and Europe. Xerxes' transgressions of natural boundaries, of course, echo the violation of social boundaries in the Candaules/queen/Gyges triangle.

The expedition moves inexorably west. Rivers are drunk dry. Bad omens are ignored, sound advice rejected. With Xerxes is the deposed Spartan king Demaratus, one of several characters in *The Histories* who fill the recurring role of the 'wise adviser'. Tell me, Xerxes bids him, will the Greeks dare to resist me? Well, says Demaratus, let me tell you about the Spartans in particular. They will fight you even if the other Greeks should surrender. Your superior numbers will be of no concern to them. If a thousand of them take the field, that thousand will fight you, and so will any number, larger or smaller.

Surely not, says Xerxes, laughing. How can this be when, unlike his subjects, they are ruled by no master? Your majesty, Demaratus replies, this is what the Spartans are like:

Fighting one on one, they are as good as any, but fighting in
formation they are the best soldiers in the world. They are free –
yes – but not entirely so; for they have a master, and that master is
Law (*Nomos*), which they fear far more than your subjects fear you.
Whatever this master commands, they do, and its command is always
the same: it is never to retreat in battle, however great the odds, but
always to maintain their positions, and either conquer or die.

Demaratus had been speaking only of the Spartans, but
Herodotus himself, in Book 5, had something to say about the
Athenians as well: when they had been ruled by the autocrats who
were known in Greece as 'tyrants' (not necessarily bad men, but
people who came to power through coups, or through their
fathers' coups), they were good fighters, but nowhere near as good
as after they got rid of the tyrants and instituted a democracy,
when as free men each person wanted to achieve something on his
own behalf.

At Demaratus's words, Xerxes laughs again (Persian laughter is
always a bad sign in Herodotus's narrative). In no way discouraged
from his enterprise, he presses on.

The first encounter would be at Thermopylae, where King
Leonidas of Sparta took his stand. With him was an advance guard
of Greeks. While they were mapping strategy, a Persian spy rode up
to assess the situation. Finding some of the Spartans stripped for
exercise and others combing their hair, he rode off in astonishment
and told Xerxes what he had seen. Don't say I didn't warn you, says
Demaratus to the mystified king. You laughed when I told you
about the Spartans, but it is their habit to pay careful attention to
their hair when they are about to risk their lives. Xerxes, however,
remains unshaken. His men attack – but to no avail. It is said,
Herodotus reports, that while watching the battle from where he
sat, Xerxes leapt to his feet three times in terror for his army. The
next day, they fight again, but the Persians cannot break the
Greeks. Xerxes, accustomed to having his way, is at a loss.

And then everything changes. A local man with his eye on a fat reward approaches Xerxes with some very interesting information. There is a hidden path over the hills up to Thermopylae. Xerxes is ecstatic. Up go the Persians. At Thermopylae, the Spartan seer Megistias examines the entrails of the sacrificial victims and announces impending doom. Deserters arrive during the night with news of the Persians' movements, and at daybreak the Greek look-outs come running from the hills. Most of the Greek troops have left. Herodotus is inclined to think that Leonidas dismissed them when he saw that they were demoralized and had no heart for the fight. Leonidas himself felt it would be unbecoming for the Spartans to desert the post they had been sent to hold, and besides, there had been an oracle to the effect that only the death of a king could preserve Sparta from destruction. And so he and his 300 Spartans stayed and fought, resisting to the last – with their swords, if they still had them, and, if not, with their hands and teeth. (Actually, only 298 were present at the end; to find out what happened to the other two, you will have to read Herodotus, and even he gives alternate versions.) Persian casualties were high as well, as Xerxes' regimental commanders urged the men ever forward, whips in hand; many fell into the sea and were drowned, and even more were trampled to death by their fellow soldiers.

Herodotus bills Thermopylae as a resounding moral victory. It not only bought time for the Greeks to the south but inspired them to resist the Persians in order to avenge Leonidas and his men. At the same time, the two fleets, Greek and Persian, fought off nearby Artemisium over a period of several days. The fighting was ultimately a stand-off, but the Greeks were encouraged to see that they could hold their own against a Persian fleet – good to know, since the next battle would take place at sea, in the straits off the island of Salamis, near Athens.

The architect of the Battle of Salamis was the brilliant Athenian politician Themistocles, who had persuaded the Athenians that the oracle they had received from Delphi about a 'wooden wall' referred not to the wooden fortifications on the Acropolis but rather to the wood of which their ships were made. Thus he persuaded them to abandon their territory to Xerxes, moving the women and children to Salamis with the idea of bringing them home after the Persians had been beaten back. It was a hard sell, and in the absence of more than a handful of defenders, Xerxes sacked the city and burned the holy places on the Acropolis. As at Thermopylae, the demoralized troops considered scattering to their homes, or at least cutting back to the Isthmus of Corinth, from which it would be comparatively easy to beat a retreat in the event of a defeat in the straits. Themistocles pre-empted disaster by sending his slave Sicinnus into the Persian camp with a message for Xerxes. Themistocles, Sicinnus reported, was really on the Persian side. The Greeks, he said,

Herodotus

> are in a state of panic and are planning retreat. If you prevent them from slipping through your fingers, you have the chance to win a glorious victory. They are at loggerheads and in no position to offer resistance. On the contrary, you will see their ships fighting among one another, the pro-Persians attacking the others.

Liking the sound of this, Xerxes encircled the Greek fleet under cover of darkness, and, bowing to the inevitable, the Greeks prepared for battle. Different combatants gave varying accounts of the course of the battle depending on both national pride and the limits of visibility, but it seemed clear to Herodotus that the ships from Athens and the nearby island of Aegina dealt enormous damage to the Persian fleet, which had fallen out of formation in the course of the battle; the Greeks awarded Athens the second prize for valour, the first going to the Aeginetans. Overall, the Greeks sustained few casualties, for if they were separated from their ships they could swim over to Salamis; Persians knocked off their ships lacked this skill and thus drowned. This time, the outcome of the naval battle was clear cut: by the end of the day, the Persians had been decisively defeated. Mardonius, understandably, feared that he would be punished for having urged the Greek war on Xerxes, and he assured the gloomy king that the loss of 'some planks of wood' would not stand in the way of an ultimate victory. Rather, the outcome of the conflict would depend, in the last analysis, on men and horses. (He does not mention the men who went down with the 'planks of wood'.) Do not lose heart, he says; sooner or later the Greeks will pay for what they have done to you. If you like, go home. I will stay here with a portion of the army and make you master of Greece.

Xerxes liked the idea of going home very much indeed, and he headed for Asia at once. Mardonius, meanwhile, offered to forgive the Athenians their past sins if they would switch sides. Panicky, the Spartans immediately dispatched envoys to dissuade the Athenians from deserting the Greek cause – and the Athenians strategically postponed giving their reply to Mardonius's envoy until the Spartans could be there to hear it. Herodotus gives full play to the stirring refusal they delivered, calculated for appreciation by friend and foe alike:

> There is not enough gold in the world or land so fair that we would accept it in exchange for collaborating with the common enemy and enslave Greece. Many powerful obstacles prevent us: first and foremost, the burning of our temples and the images of our gods. We consider it our duty to avenge this desecration with might and main, and not to enter into a treaty with its perpetrator. And then too there is the fact that we are all Greeks, one race speaking a single language, with shrines and sacrifices in common, a similar way of life. We wish you to know, then, if you do not know it already, that as long as a single Athenian remains alive, we will never come to terms with Xerxes.

And so Mardonius lingered in Greece and faced the combined Greek forces under the Spartan Pausanias, regent for Leonidas's underage son Pleistarchus. The two armies met at Plataea, near Thebes, the following spring. As was customary before a battle in the ancient world, both commanders took the omens before engaging battle, and for both, the omens were bad. Pausanias, however, managed at the last moment to secure a favourable sign as the battle was virtually being engaged, and the Greeks were in fact victorious. They owed their victory in no small part to the structure of the Persian military – Persian resistance collapsed when Mardonius was killed – as well as to the Persians' lack of armour, for without it, they could not hold up against hoplites. Herodotus makes a point of saying that the Persians were in no way lacking in courage; he will not stoop to belittle Xerxes' formidable soldiers.

6. This small bowl, known as a kylix, shows a hoplite, bearing a shield with a Pegasus motif, towering over a Persian dressed in garb the Greeks would have found outlandish. It is the work of an artist known as the Triptolemus Painter, c. 460 BC. Herodotus did not portray Persians as quite so ridiculous

Rumour had it that it was on the very same day that the Greek fleet prevailed against the Persians at Mycale in Ionia: 'the divine ordering of things', Herodotus wrote, 'is made clear by many proofs', not least of which was the divinely aided report of the victory at Plataea that reached Mycale just as battle was about to be engaged, a development that gave a powerful boost to the Greeks' morale. With the Persians' defeat at Mycale, their attempt to conquer the Greeks came to an inglorious end. The unthinkable had happened. A band of small, poor Greek states, acting in concert to defend their homeland, had triumphed over the wealthy Persian king and his host of, literally, millions.

This is indeed the celebratory martial tune that Herodotus has presented for our delectation, complete with recurrent motifs (the exhortations before battle, the catalogues of daring deeds, the fatal discounting of the wise adviser or divine signs, the superiority of Greek ways of thinking to Persian ones). It reaches one high point in the Spartan stand at Thermopylae and a second at the victory at Salamis. If we think of it as a piece for piano rather than as a symphony, however, we have to ask what the left hand is doing while the right hand is producing the unforgettable major chords that still resound *fortissimo* today. And the answer is a subtle counterpoint without which the joyfully triumphal melody risks ringing sentimental, even tinny.

For even the most casual reading of Herodotus's narrative makes plain his awareness that the Greeks were anything but united in defending their homeland. More Greeks fought for Xerxes than fought against him. Among the allied states, ambivalence and apathy were widespread. Miltiades had an uphill fight persuading the Athenian commanders to engage the Persians at Marathon. The Spartans sent only a small force to Thermopylae, and their allies were so skittish that Leonidas was evidently nervous about having them around. On the eve of Salamis, Themistocles threatened to put all the Athenians on board their ships and sail away to Italy if the Spartan commander Eurybiades would not agree to fight in the straits rather than pulling back to the Isthmus; even after persuading Eurybiades, he viewed the situation as so dicey that he was willing to provoke a Persian blockade in order to force a battle. The following spring, the Spartans thought twice about acceding to the Athenians' request for help at Plataea. In fact, they seriously considered walling the Isthmus that separated their territory from that of the Athenians and abandoning them to their fate. And the Athenians' showy protestations of undying loyalty to Greece were balanced by far darker words almost immediately afterwards, when they dropped hints to the Spartans that if they did not get moving, then they might have to reconsider accepting the Persians' terms. So much for Greek solidarity.

Nor are the Persians portrayed in an entirely unflattering light. Herodotus depicts them as fighting bravely at Plataea, and the sycophantic and manipulative Mardonius is balanced by the courageous and far-sighted Artabanus, who in many ways reprises with Xerxes the role Solon had played with Croesus. Herodotus takes pain to humanize even Xerxes, whose initial anxieties about invading Greece he highlights as the king begins to get cold feet the night after announcing his intentions to his councillors – and is then terrified by a phantom who appears in a series of dreams threatening him about the consequences if he fails to follow through. En route to Greece, moreover, when he pauses to survey his forces, the sight of the Hellespont completely covered by his ships and the land nearby teeming with his soldiers at first delights him. He calls himself happy – and promptly bursts into tears. Artabanus, whom Xerxes had not punished by keeping him back in Persia with the women after all, inquires as to this sudden change of mood. 'I was reflecting on things', Xerxes replies, 'and it came into my mind how pitifully short human life is – for out of all this multitude not one will be alive a hundred years from now'. This time, when Artabanus replies with a disquisition on the uncontrollable vicissitudes of human life, Xerxes does not get angry; rather, he acknowledges that Artabanus has described the human condition rather well. Even Xerxes has his moments in *The Histories*.

Finally, the twin victories of Plataea and Mycale are not the last we hear of the Greeks' interactions with Persia. After the battle at Mycale, the Athenians, under their commander Xanthippus, lay siege to Sestos, the most formidable Persian stronghold in the area now known as the Gallipoli peninsula. The local governor Artaÿctes, we learn, was a dreadful man who had stolen vast amounts of votive offerings from the sanctuary of the Trojan War hero Protesilaus in nearby Elaeus – money, cups of gold and silver – and, worse still, would take women into the sanctuary and have sex with them, something strictly forbidden by Greek norms. When Sestos finally falls, Artaÿctes offers large sums of money in exchange for his life and that of his son. Xanthippus, however, refuses the money. The people of Elaeus want revenge for the desecration of the sanctuary and demand Artaÿctes' execution, and Xanthippus is inclined this way himself. And so the Athenians nail him to a plank of wood – and stone his son to death before his eyes.

There are nearly a thousand named characters in *The Histories*, and Artaÿctes is just one of them. Forget his name and the story retains its meaning. The name of Protesilaus, though, whose shrine Artaÿctes had violated, is a nice touch of ring composition, bringing us back as it does to the origins of the Trojan War with which *The Histories* began, and Xanthippus, as any Greek would know, was not just any Greek general: he was father to Pericles, the architect of Athenian imperialism. Readers may also be reminded of an earlier incident in *The Histories* when the Persian Oroetes hung Polycrates of Samos on a cross; now it is the Greeks who are doing the crucifying. *The Histories*, then, concludes on an ominous note. For the expected celebratory coda Herodotus has substituted what a musicologist might call a 'deceptive cadence': instead of the final chord we are expecting, we get something jarring and unexpected, leaving us at the very least up in the air, and at the most deeply anxious about what may lie ahead.

Herodotus has always remained our chief source for the Persian Wars. Each battle he recounted has had its champions; John Stuart Mill famously suggested that 'the Battle of Marathon, even as an event in English history, is more important than the Battle of Hastings'. Strong words, these. Pride of place, however, has generally been given not to any of the stunning Greek victories but rather to the world-famous defeat at Thermopylae, for it is always comforting to feel that one could recast a total wipe-out as a voluntary sacrifice for the sake of the nation. As Montaigne wrote in 1580, 'there are triumphant defeats that rival victories', and none of the Greeks' victories against Persia could compare in glory with the Spartans' annihilation at Thermopylae.

The Thermopylae legend was a particularly powerful mantra in the run-up to the liberation of Greece from Turkish domination in the 1820s. Already in 1737, Richard Glover had made quite a splash with his epic poem *Leonidas*, which recounted the events surrounding the battle; *Leonidas* was translated from English into French, German, and Danish. Glover's sequel, *The Athenaid*, offered a telling variant on Herodotus's account of Leonidas's death: although Herodotus had reported that Xerxes stuck the dead Leonidas's head on a pole, Glover pointedly has the Spartan king crucified by this enemy of civilization, thus evoking the parallel death of Jesus and the notion of voluntary self-sacrifice. David painted his famous *Leonidas at Thermopylae* in 1814. Byron was in a long tradition when he wrote his famous lines:

> Must we but weep o'er days more blest?
> Must we but blush? – Our fathers bled.
> Earth! Render back from out thy breast
> A remnant of our Spartan dead!
> Of the three hundred grant but three,
> To make a new Thermopylae!

7. This lithograph by Arthur A. Dixon shows Lord Byron being welcomed in 1823 at Messolonghi, Greece, where he had gone to support the Greek war of independence against the Ottoman Turks; the poet died there of a fever a year later, the city still under siege

Several years after the Ottoman yoke had finally been shaken off, Andreas Koromilas published the first modern Greek translation of Herodotus as an inspiration to his countrymen.

The Thermopylae motif was often invoked to add historical context to a last-ditch effort to hold off vastly superior numbers. Thus the remarkable success of a hastily assembled force of Indian and British troops in forcing the invading Japanese to retreat from the Indian township of Kohima in 1944 – a significant turning point in World War II – was labelled by Mountbatten 'the British/Indian Thermopylae'. A familiar epitaph carved there entreats its readers:

> When you go home, tell them of us and say,
> For their tomorrow, we gave our today.

It is difficult not to believe that these lines, probably the work of the English classicist John Maxwell Edmonds (1875–1958), were not modelled on the epitaph for the Thermopylae dead attributed to Simonides and quoted by Herodotus:

> Go tell the Spartans, stranger passing by,
> That here, obeying their commands, we lie.

Curiously, the Thermopylae motif was invoked not only in defensive contexts but in offensive ones as well. The hapless Germans sent to suffer miserably during the futile siege of Stalingrad were not charmed to receive these same commands coming from Hitler – to fight to the death rather than surrender – and they were positively horrified to learn that the European press was spreading Göring's claim that they were willingly sacrificing themselves to save civilization from the onslaught of barbarian hordes from the East just as the Spartans had done over two millennia earlier.

In the United States, the decisive defeat of the American forces at the Alamo in 1836 gave birth to a memorial bearing the words

8. The Alamo in San Antonio, Texas, is still a popular tourist destination today

'Thermopylae had her messenger of defeat – the Alamo had none', and the unsuccessful defence of a Confederate outpost at Sabine Pass in Texas in 1863 prompted a book entitled *Sabine Pass: The Confederacy's Thermopylae*. A century later, the Americans began sending troops to Vietnam, and in 1978 Daniel Ford's novel about that war, *Incident at Muc Wa*, was made into a film entitled *Go Tell the Spartans*. Starring Burt Lancaster and Craig Wasson, the movie shaped itself around the theme of voluntary sacrifice and organized its plot around the defence of Thermopylae.

When the Americans arrive at the little outpost of Muc Wa in 1963, they find a graveyard with 300 bodies and an epitaph inscribed over the entrance in French. Young Wasson recognizes it as the Simonides epitaph and translates it for a puzzled comrade who has no idea what to make of it. Familiarity with Thermopylae is thus portrayed as the mark of an educated man who knows his history (and his French). The Americans at Muc Wa refuse to believe that they can fail as the French had, but they are betrayed:

47

it is stressed that several roads lead into their camp. Unlike Leonidas, Burt Lancaster, who has seen much of war and become cynical in the extreme, has no desire to stay once the cause is plainly lost, and he need not, for unlike the Spartans, the Americans have helicopters. The film's turning point comes when Lancaster abandons the evacuation helicopter and joins the idealistic Wasson in fighting in defence of their hopeless position. When the sun rises after a horrible night battle, we see Lancaster's corpse lying naked in the marshy ground. Wasson staggers into the French graveyard, not mortally wounded, it seems, but without the best prospects for making his way back to safety. The Spartans at Thermopylae bought time for Greece; the Americans at Muc Wa died for nothing.

Helped along by later authors who drew heavily on his work and, of course, by Simonides' epitaph, which was available for incorporation into *The Histories*, Herodotus not only gave us the legend of Thermopylae, the centrepiece of his war epic, but also reinforced the very notion of the war monograph as the long, grand story *par excellence*, an idea taken over from Homer and passed on to Thucydides and countless others. Herodotus's account of the wars reprises the same themes we see elsewhere in *The Histories*: wondrous deeds worthy of remembrance, the fragility of human happiness, but also the endemic nature of imperial ambition. And the gods' role in all this? Herodotus clearly believes them to play some part, a theme we will revisit in Chapter 6.

Chapter 4

Herodotus as ethnographer

There are no mules in Elis.

The Atlantes never dream.

The Getae think they're immortal.

The Scythians gild their dead fathers' skulls. And feast on their flesh.

In Egypt women urinate standing up, but men squat.

In the Caucasus, it is said, people copulate in public like animals.

The Babylonians bury their dead in honey.

The Gyzantes eat monkeys!

All this Herodotus gleaned from inquiries carried out in the course of his travels. In Book 1, he tells of the customs practised in Lydia and Persia; Book 2 is devoted in its entirety to Egypt; Book 3 includes Cambyses' violation of accepted norms in Egypt, Darius's experiment to see how different peoples react to one another's ways of dealing with the dead, and Herodotus's treatment of the ends of the earth. Book 4 deals with Scythia and, briefly, Libya. Beginning with Book 5, the focus shifts to more narrow political history, though not without some important ethnographic diversions – the customs of the Spartans, for example, which offer surprising parallels to those of non-Greek peoples.

Ethnography can be seen as made up of two key features that blend existentially: perspective and methodology. An ethnographer must be both humanist and scientist – humanist in the ability to transcend his or her own culture and evaluate other societies in a non-judgemental framework, scientist in the gathering of evidence through observation and interview. In both areas, Herodotus's natural curiosity and energy led him to pioneer a new field that would greatly broaden his fellow Greeks' understanding of the human community and eventually lay the foundation for European anthropologists working in the new world.

Just as authors of science fiction use their alternative worlds to make statements about the one in which they live, part of Herodotus's purpose was to highlight what was distinctively Greek by setting forth customs that were distinctly un-Greek. Though Herodotus shows unusual open-mindedness about the customs of non-Greek peoples, both 'civilized' such as the Egyptians and the Persians and 'uncivilized' such as the Scythians, he tends to see them through Greek eyes – but not always: Herodotus's cultural map is not grounded in a simple binary opposition. A man who could think only in terms of either/or could not have written *The Histories*.

The notion that cultural norms varied over time and space was hotly contested in Herodotus's day (though few Greeks suspected, as Herodotus did, that some foreign ways might be better than their own). Did the gods really exist, some wondered, or had people made them up? If you didn't like a law, could you just change it, or was there some kind of underlying natural principle that would cry out against this? It all boiled down to *nomos* versus *physis*. The Greek word *nomos* embraced several different ideas: legal enactment, socially reinforced norm, value, custom, habit. The *physis* (nature) champions saw some things as right, others as wrong, and considered this distinction eternal and non-negotiable. *Nomos* people took a different view. For them, rules were man-made and could be changed – or ignored. *Nomoi*, of course, are precisely the sorts of things that interest ethnographers. Who makes the rules among these people, and what are the penalties for their violation? What do they respect? How do they spend their days? What about sex? Marriage?

Child-rearing? How do they handle death? Who eats what; why? *Physis* may be of some interest as well – climate, for example, might shape individuals and cultures – but *nomos* takes pride of place.

Nomos was of particular interest to Herodotus's contemporaries the sophists, who revelled in exposing what they considered the arbitrariness of it all and, like some of Socrates' peskier interlocutors, encouraged their followers to believe that laws were made to be broken. Herodotus, however, took the opposing view: in *The Histories*, he shows us the primacy of reverence for varying *nomoi*. One can ignore *nomoi*, certainly; they are not laws like the laws of nature – of *physis*. But one does so at one's peril. The most famous case in *The Histories* is that of Cyrus's son Cambyses, who mocked the Egyptians for worshipping the calf known as Apis and indeed dealt Apis a fatal wound in the thigh. This act horrified not only the Egyptians but Herodotus as well. We are left to believe that it is no coincidence that Cambyses died from a wound in precisely the same spot in which he had previously wounded Apis. In the context of Cambyses' mad disregard of local *nomoi*, Herodotus tells a now famous tale about an experiment undertaken by Darius to demonstrate the universal preference for one's native customs:

> Darius invited some Greeks who were present to a conference and asked them how much money he would have to pay them to eat the bodies of their dead fathers. They replied that no amount of money would get them to do this. Next the king summoned some members of the Callatiae, an Indian tribe who eat their dead parents, and asked them in the presence of the Greeks – an interpreter being there so that they could understand what was being said – how much money it would take for them to agree to cremate their fathers' bodies. They cried out in horror and forbade him to say such ghastly things. And so these practices have become enshrined as enduring customs, and I believe Pindar was right to have said in his poem that custom is king of all.

Yet the Greek Herodotus himself rarely expresses revulsion from any of the vast array of non-Greek customs he encounters. Like the sophists, he took *nomoi* for the most part as they came, and as a proper field worker, he aspired to the role of recorder, not judge. To the north, there are these people, and they have these customs, and their flora and fauna are thus; across the mountains are these people, and they have these customs, and these flora and fauna; and they say that across the desert are these people, with these customs, and the following flora and fauna. Like modern anthropologists, he was a cultural relativist, but only up to a point: he does periodically pause to praise or condemn. In his few condemnations, he is still on higher ground than some of his successors; even a highly esteemed field worker like Bronislaw Malinowski said far harsher things in his memoirs about the objects of his research than anything we read in Herodotus.

In addition to his curiosity about varying *nomoi*, Herodotus was interested in differing *nomoi* about *nomoi*. The Persians, he tells us, adopt more foreign customs than any other people. Contrast with these the Egyptians, who stick to their ancestral *nomoi* and never adopt any new ones. Two very long stories tell of individuals whose enthusiasm for foreign ways led to their deaths: Anacharsis the Scythian, who was evidently killed by his brother when his involvement in a foreign religious cult was discovered, and Scyles, another Scythian, who, having become enamoured of Greek culture, began sneaking around in Greek clothing and worshipping the Greek gods: when somebody snitched, his brother too brought about his death. 'So conservative are the Scythians', Herodotus concludes, 'that they treat people who adopt foreign customs in this way'.

Like most ethnographers, Herodotus deemed the minutiae of everyday life well worth recording. In his work, however, the daily customs and practices of others are by their very strangeness transmuted into the exotic. Here he set himself apart from modern ethnographers and anthropologists, who are trained to curb their enthusiasms and simply record what they see or hear. Lacking in *The Histories* is the crisp and controlled stance of the professional field worker; Herodotus's observations about the worlds he visits are distinctive by virtue of being shot through with wonder. *You are never going to believe this*, we read as a continual subtext.

At times more like a travel writer than an ethnographer, Herodotus was constantly drawn to the remarkable, the bizarre, the unusual, the fantastic, the macabre – anything that differed dramatically from what he and his fellow Greeks were accustomed to. He delighted in the 'far-out' – literally and figuratively (he was enthralled by what lay at the ends of the known world, like the Indian ants bigger than foxes who dug up gold from the ground) – partly because of a characterological fascination with the extraordinary, partly because of his commitment to full and accurate reporting, but partly too, no doubt, because he knew it made good copy.

Herodotus was particularly fond of unusual phenomena that illustrated the resourcefulness of humankind. Take the ingenuity of the Scythians: when they have sacrificed an ox, they face a challenge in cooking it, since there is no wood in Scythia with which to make a fire, nor are cauldrons always available. Consequently, they put all the flesh into the ox's paunch, mix some water with it, and boil it over a fire they have made from the bones; lo, a self-cooking ox! In Arabia, large birds bring sticks of cinnamon to nests on mountain precipices so high that no man can climb up to get them, and so the Arabians have developed the following strategy: they cut up the bodies of beasts of burden into very large joints and leave them near the nests. The birds then fly down and carry the joints up to their nests – but the nests are not strong enough to bear the weight, and when they break and fall to the ground, the Arabians step in and retrieve the cinnamon, which they then export to other lands. And there's more: one sort of sheep in Arabia has flat tails eighteen inches across, astonishing enough but not problematic. The other sort presents a challenge, for their tails are so long – four and a half feet or more – that they would get sore from being dragged along the ground if the sheep were allowed to trail them behind as they walked. But the shepherds, it seems, know enough about woodworking to make little carts and affix one under the tail of each sheep. Problem solved!

Herodotus is plainly delighted by the system the men of Babylon found to ensure that all their women were properly married off: unmarried daughters are a much more serious problem than tender tails. Every year, the Babylonians held a gathering in which the young women were put up for auction in descending order of pulchritude: the wealthiest men would outbid one another for the privilege of marrying the prettiest women, and the money thus collected would be used to provide dowries for the least attractive females as well as the handicapped ones, if there were any. Thus everyone went home married and with nothing to complain of. Once more: problem solved! And better still: the achievement of balance, something very important to Herodotus.

Altogether, the huge and wealthy city of Babylon struck Herodotus with wonder, but the second greatest wonder he reports finding there were the boats that plied the Euphrates down to the city. The current of the river was too strong for boats to sail north on it, but the merchants found a way around this. Upstream of Babylon, in Armenia, they constructed boats with no prow or stern; they were round, like a shield, with watertight skins stretched across a frame of willow. Having laden them with cargo, they placed on them two men to steer them, as well as one or more donkeys, depending on the size of the boat. When the men have reached Babylon and sold their cargo, they sell the frame of the boat, load the donkeys up with the skins, and drive them north back to Armenia. Once they have arrived in Armenia with the donkeys, they build new frames and start the boat-building process again. Thus trade can be conducted without boats needing to sail against the current. Another problem solved.

His fascination with diversity prompts Herodotus to share with us the distinguishing eating habits of the peoples he has studied. Three clans in Babylon eat nothing but fish. Most of the tribes who inhabit the Caucasus live off wild scrub. The Callipidae eat grain, onions, garlic, lentils, and millet. The peace-loving Argippaeans, who are bald from birth, eat entirely from the fruit of the *pontikos* tree, from which they make both food and drink. Those Ethiopians who live in caves eat snakes and lizards. The women of Cyrene will not eat the flesh of cows out of reverence for the Egyptian cow-goddess Isis. And, of course, the Gyzantes eat monkeys.

As is the case with anthropological works today, gender roles and marriage more inevitably come in for a particularly large share of attention in *The Histories*. Like modern ethnographers, Herodotus recognizes the shock value of customs that fly in the face of traditional Western values of patriarchy, with its determined control of female sexuality and the attendant division into public and private. In Babylon, to Herodotus's horror, every woman must once in her life go sit in the temple of Aphrodite and have sex with the first man who throws her a coin; only then may she get on with her life, which is invariably one of sexual propriety. (Tall, good-looking women get home quickly enough, but some of the less prepossessing ones have to keep trying for as long as three or four years.) The women of the Gindanes wear an anklet for each man with whom they have had sex, and the woman with the most anklets is considered to be the most outstanding, since she has been loved by the most men. Rather than pairing off in couples, the Ausees have sex promiscuously, like animals, and when the babies who result from this intercourse are grown, they are brought before a meeting of the men and assigned a father on the basis of physical resemblance.

Most fully developed is Herodotus's treatment of the Amazons, which differs radically from other ancient narratives in its admiring portrayal of these warrior women. It is also a great story.

Notorious gender-benders, the Amazons were regularly depicted by Greeks as freakish enemies of civilization; on the Parthenon friezes that commemorated the Greek victories in the Persian Wars, dangerous forces of nature are signalled by the dual portrayal of Amazons and the half-human, half-equine centaurs. The orator Lysias, a couple of generations younger than Herodotus, boasted of the early Athenians' victory over them in war. In *The Histories*, however, we encounter a charming play-by-play account of the courtship of the Amazons and the Scythians that culminates in the happy marriage of the two groups, resulting down the line in the people known as the Sarmatians. None of the gruesome details about the Amazons we encounter elsewhere (such as their habit of putting their male babies to death) has any place in Herodotus's narrative.

About the Sarmatians, Herodotus reports, the following tale is told. Having fought with some formidable soldiers whom ships had carried to their shores, the Scythians are surprised to learn from an examination of the corpses of the vanquished that they were women. Taking counsel, they determine to stop fighting them but rather to take a stab at making friends, hoping to have children from such redoubtable mothers. A contingent of Scythian youth is sent out with instructions to camp near these strange women. Little by little, the Amazons and the Scythians encamp closer and closer to one another. At midday, the Amazons were in the habit of scattering at a distance from one another, one by one or in twos, evidently (though the Greek is obscure) for bathroom purposes, and the Scythians, who have carefully been mimicking their every move, do the same – hardly a traditional activity for a first date, but this is what Herodotus seems to say. When one of the Scythians then approaches one of the Amazons with amorous intentions, the woman readily agrees, and indeed indicates to him in sign language that he should return the following day with a friend and she will do the same. (This gets better and better.) Not long afterwards, the two groups pair off completely and join their camps into one. After a while, the Scythians suggest to the

Amazons that they all return to the main body of their people, where their parents and possessions are. The plucky Amazons, however, will have none of it. For us to live with your women is unworkable, they reply,

> for we don't have the same customs that they do. We shoot bows and throw javelins and ride horses, but we never learnt to do housework, whereas your women do none of the things that we do; they stay inside the wagons and do women's work. They never go hunting – in fact, they never go anywhere. We could never get along with them. But if you want us to be your wives and you really want to play fair, go get your share of your property from your parents, and then we'll make a community of our own together.

Astonishingly, the young men agree, and off they go, three days' journey east and three days north, and establish their new society, which became the Sarmatians. The Sarmatian women to Herodotus's day continued to ride out hunting on horseback and fighting in war. No Sarmatian woman, moreover, can marry until she has killed an enemy, and for this reason – in an interesting mirroring of the plight of the less attractive women sitting for years in the temple at Babylon – some of them die of old age still unmarried.

Much of the data Herodotus shares with us not only concern non-Greek and therefore noteworthy customs but also outline a distinct life cycle of sex, marriage, food, and death. All these take place in a social context: sexual mores lead ultimately to childbirth; the newly created human must follow group norms in its eating habits and, again, sexual life; and in time, he or she will undergo a socially sanctioned funeral and burial (or the lack of them): sometimes the traditions of the group will actually bring about the deaths of its individuals, and always they will determine what is done with bodies after death.

Few of us would want to live among the Padaean Indians. Even if we could tolerate their diet of raw flesh, we might think twice if the flesh being served up were ours: whenever Padaeans fall ill, Herodotus reports, their closest associates of the same sex put them to death lest their flesh spoil and become unsuitable for eating; meanwhile, the patients deny vigorously that they are ill. (The comic potential is great: we can easily envision a Padaean sitting up in protest… 'No, really, I'm feeling much better today!') For all their insistence, still they are killed and their flesh doled out for a feast. The tribe sacrifices and eats anyone who grows to old age, but hardly anyone ever does, of course, since to read *The Histories* one imagines that their friends and relations make away with them at the first sign of a sniffle.

In his discussion of the Padaeans, Herodotus links death and eating; it is death and sex/marriage that are paired in his treatment of the Thracians who live north of Crestonia. They practise polygyny, it seems, and when a man dies, his wives are subjected to elaborate tests to determine which one he loved the most. The lucky winner, after hearing her praises sung by men and women alike, has her throat cut over her husband's tomb by her nearest relative, and she is then buried with him. The others feel that they have suffered a huge misfortune, for nothing is considered more worthy of reproach than not having been chosen.

Herodotus's account of the Massagetae, on the other hand, manages to roll sex/marriage, death, and eating into one neat account. The Massagetae are milk drinkers and have no agriculture, eating only meat and fish. Although each man marries a single wife, they all share their wives with one another, and they determine the proper time to die in the following way:

> When someone reaches an advanced age, the family throws a party and includes him in a general sacrifice of cattle; then they boil and eat the flesh. They hold this to be the best kind of death. Those who die of disease, on the other hand, are not eaten but rather buried, and it is considered a great calamity not to live long enough to be sacrificed.

The Issedones do something similar, only with the bodies of those who are already dead. When a man's father has died, all his relatives bring cattle to his house. Sacrificing the animals and cutting the meat into pieces, they then also chop up their host's dead father and make a banquet out of the mixed meats. In addition, they pluck the hair from the head of the dead man, clean it out, and gild it.

It is true that Herodotus did not assemble his varied data sufficiently to get at the heart of what made a society tick. He tells us a great deal about the rituals of the peoples he discusses – burial rites, animal sacrifice, the occasional human sacrifice – but almost nothing about their belief systems. He did not stay in any one place long enough to become a master of its ethos, and for this he is often taken to task as not practising 'real' ethnography – for being really nothing more than a tourist. He did not fully adopt the role of 'participant observer', settling among a people for the traditional anthropological minimum stay of a year and seeking to blend in with his surroundings even as he devoted himself to interviewing native informants. Kapuściński tells how he shared hashish with some people he met in Sudan; Herodotus reports that the Scythians got high on cannabis, 'howling with pleasure', but nowhere suggests that he himself partook of the experience. Of course, modern anthropologists delude themselves when they imagine they have effaced their identity and become one with 'their' people, but they at least go through the motions. And Herodotus was no doubt just as vulnerable as modern ethnographers to lying informants who took no end of pleasure in pulling a sober inquirer's leg.

His linguistic limitations not only left him at the mercy of interpreters and the minority of Greek-speaking locals – hardly a representative bunch – but stamped him indelibly as an outsider. One is reminded of the observations of Kapuściński, who writes that there must have been something in my appearance and gestures, in my way of sitting and moving, that gave me away – betrayed where I came from, from how different a world. I sensed that they took me for an alien.... I began to feel unpleasant and uncomfortable. I had changed my suit, but I apparently could not conceal whatever lay beneath it that had shaped and marked me out as a foreign particle.

And this was only in Rome, a stopover en route from Poland to India! We learn, too, from Kapuściński how one of the locals took him up to the top of a mosque to show him the view – and then demanded that he hand over his money. Did Herodotus have experiences like this? If he did, we never learn about them. What did the objects of his study make of him? Did he stay in private homes, help with household chores – or not help? It's not hard to imagine the muttering: 'He's a lot of fun, but would it kill him to pick up a scythe once in a while?'

Inevitably, Herodotus was somewhat prone to falling into generalization. It was easy for him to seize on individual details he had observed and extrapolate wildly. One can see him in Britain: 'England being a very cold country, the Londoners live on a food they call curry, eating it all day long, for it makes their entire bodies feel warm, and when they begin to feel cold again, they eat some more. This food they get from India, and it is carried from there on the backs of the dogs one sees all over Britain. This, it seems to me, must be the reason for the great affection the Britons bestow on dogs.' If we are going to complain that Herodotus did not in all respects come up to the standards of modern ethnographers, however, we should also censure Alexander Graham Bell for not having invented the mobile phone and Thomas Edison for not having invented the microwave oven. And we should bear in mind the serious doubts cast upon Margaret Mead's famous ethnography *Coming of Age in Samoa*, doubts that have gained credibility from the fact that she never learned the language and relied on local English-speakers. Most of all, we should remember that Herodotus never laid aside his scepticism.

He is fully aware of the unreliability even of his informants' most dearly held beliefs: each of the Neuroi, he tells us, is said by the Scythians to become a wolf for a few days each year and then return to his original form. 'I myself', he reports, 'do not believe them when they say this, but nonetheless, they do say it, and indeed swear to it'. He is amused by the citizens of the twelve cities of Ionia who claimed to be of purest Ionian descent; even the colonists who began in the very town hall of Athens, he argues, took no wives with them but married local Carian girls whose parents they had killed.

Despite what we moderns perceive as a lack of depth in getting at the core values of any people he has visited, he is plainly intrigued by the many parallels – and contrasts – that he discovers in the wide spectrum that makes up the human community. The Babylonians' dirges for the dead are like those in use in Egypt. The people of Cyprus have an institution similar to the practice that kept unattractive Babylonian girls sitting hopefully in the temple of Aphrodite for three or four years. The Spartans resemble the Egyptians in that a young man will move out of the way if he sees an older man approaching; professions in both societies, moreover, are handed down from father to son, such that a fluteplayer is the son of a fluteplayer, a cook of a cook, and the herald of a herald. Spartan practices regarding the death of their kings parallel those of the Persians: when the king has died and another has been appointed, the new king of Sparta frees all who were debtors to the king or to the state, and the Persian king remits to the various cities the arrears of any tribute that was due. Except for the Nasamones, who bury dead bodies in a sitting posture (taking care not to let anyone die lying down!), the nomads bury the dead just as the Greeks do.

Contrasts are key to the notion of ethnography. Distinctive practices can help define what makes a society unique, and, perhaps more important still, great contrasts make great stories. For the ethnographer, as we have seen, is not only voyeur,

9. There was no limit to Herodotus's appetite for things Egyptian

although Herodotus certainly adopts this role (an ironic one, in view of the value placed in the Gyges tale on looking only on one's own); he or she is also exhibitionist. For all the professional protocol that calls for regarding alien customs with equanimity, it is hard not to cry out, 'See what I found! Look at this! Isn't it amazing! Not like anything we've seen before, is it?' Herodotus's presentation of the 'upside-down' customs of Egypt, a land where even the river flows backwards, is always included when 'Herodotus's greatest hits' are assigned in schools.

Nearly all Egyptian practices, Herodotus tells us, are the opposite of those found everywhere else in the world. Women buy and sell in the marketplace, while men stay home to attend to the weaving. Women stand to urinate, while men squat. Sons are not compelled to support their parents (this was the law in Athens), but daughters are. Greeks write from left to right, Egyptians from right to left, and the Egyptians, not surprisingly, say that it is the Greeks who write backwards. Others (if they have not been influenced by the Egyptians) leave the genitals in their natural state, but the Egyptians practise circumcision. Elsewhere priests wear their hair long, but Egyptian priests shave their heads. Among most peoples the head is shaved during periods of mourning, but the Egyptians let both their head hair and their beards grow. (Herodotus has a marked interest in hair. The Babylonians, we learn, wear their hair long and wrap their heads in turbans. The Arabians cut their hair all around in a circle, shaving their temples, in imitation, they say, of Dionysus. The Macai shave their hair so as to leave tufts, letting the hair grow long in the middle but shaving it close to the skin on the sides.)

Inevitably, Herodotus's picture of the Egyptians is over-schematized. We suspect some of his informants were less than honest with him. Women were not the sole retailers in Egyptian families; circumcision was not practised universally among the Egyptians; Greeks as well as Egyptians urinated and defaecated indoors. Yet it is precisely Herodotus's determination to set up these oppositions that reveals his commitment to uncovering the remarkable cultural diversity of the human community and sharing it with his audience. Not all of those inspired by his work to seek out this diversity shared his enthusiasm for it: the writer and artist James Forbes, born in London in 1749 but resident in India from 1765 to 1784, was inspired by Herodotus's work and drew parallels between Brahmin and ancient Egyptian purification rites, but differed markedly from Herodotus in perspective: in 1810, he issued a call for the conversion of Hindus to Christianity.

Setting out divergences between Greeks and non-Greeks is a central part of Herodotus's agenda. Yet the many contrasts and parallels he retails make plain that he by no means sees the world as divided into Greek and Other. Perhaps the most striking example comes in Darius's unsuccessful invasion of Scythia in Book 4, the occasion for Herodotus's long account of Scythian history and mores. For compared to the Scythians, the invading Persians seem quite normal – those same Persians whom the

Greeks perceive as an odd people in strange clothing, made soft by wealth and having no problem with a ridiculous system of government that makes an entire nation slaves of a potentially capricious monarch. These same Persians, however, have fixed homes; they build cities; they sow crops. The Scythians, on the other hand, are nomads, a poor people constantly on the move in wagons that substitute for houses. Their perpetual motion drives Darius to distraction, for he cannot pin them down in battle, and eventually he is forced to go home empty-handed. Well, not quite; he does manage to conquer Thrace, useful as a bulkhead for an invasion of Europe. But against Scythia he is powerless. The Scythians' very lack of 'civilized' ways makes them impossible to defeat. They are mystifying even in their mode of communication, sending him a gift of a bird, a mouse, a frog, and five arrows, and leaving it to the king and his councillors to try to decode this obscure message. For the more conventional Scythians, of course – not the ones who mate with the strange women – it is the Amazons who are Other (imagine women hunting and going to war!), but for the Persians it is the Scythians. And to bring these polarities full circle, we might say that the evasive Scythians in their wagons are not entirely unlike the Athenians – also at that time a poor people – who flee the Persians by taking to their wooden walls and decamping for Salamis.

Herodotus set out to memorialize the wondrous deeds of both Greeks and non-Greeks, but in dealing with these two sets of peoples, he found that they did not form monolithic blocs. Dramatic differences divided not only the various groups of 'barbarians' but also the Greeks themselves, as witness the Spartans, whose customs sometimes parallel barbarian customs and are thus inevitably of interest to the man Kapuściński called 'the first globalist'. In *The Histories*, Herodotus combines large ideas – the sanctity of *nomos*, the possibility of departures from patriarchal norms, the mind-boggling multiplicity of human pathways – with a wealth of detail. Because such details fascinate him, he makes them fascinating to us.

Chapter 5

Women in history, women in *The Histories*

In light of the prominence accorded to women in the ethnographies, it is no surprise that they also play large roles elsewhere in the narrative. Women, after all, were front and centre in the epic tales that played such a large role in the shaping of Herodotus's work. In the *Iliad*, we find Helen, the *casus belli*; the captive maidens Chryseis and Briseis, war's playthings; Andromache and Hecuba, Hector's forceful wife and his mother. The *Odyssey* sports a diverse collection of memorable females who alternately assist and impede the hero's return to his faithful wife Penelope – the nymph Calypso, who keeps him for seven years on her island; the witch Circe, who turns his men into pigs; the seductive Sirens; but also the helpful princess Nausicaä, and finally the goddess Athena, who comes to Odysseus's rescue when she senses danger. And it ends with the demise of the unlucky household maids, who had slept with Penelope's infamous suitors under constraint – and are hanged for it by Odysseus on his return.

Women are ubiquitous in *The Histories* as well. Herodotean scholar Carolyn Dewald has counted 375 mentions of women or femaleness in Herodotus's work. The roles of females in *The Histories* are extraordinarily diverse, ranging from impalers to kidnapping victims, from queens to slaves, from hydraulic engineers to precocious girls. Women pull men together in marriage alliances and drive them apart in family strife; they kill and are killed; they rescue some relatives and destroy others. We could not expect less, for at the outset of his work, after all, Herodotus proclaimed his goal of preserving the memory of what people have done; of the most marvellous things that have happened; and, most particularly, of everything that has transpired pertaining to the war between the Greeks and the Persians. There was no way he could do this without a breadth of vision that would encompass both sexes, and would explore each in a wide variety of functions.

Women make their first appearance at the very outset of *The Histories* when Herodotus begins to narrate the series of purported abductions that, according to the Persians, culminated in the Trojan War, and indeed the long-standing feud between East and West. But Herodotus recounts this tit-for-tat interpretation of history at a distance, balancing the Persian version with a Phoenician account and throwing in a Greek variant as well. Women, he seems to say, have been the subjects of many titillating tales told by men, and people certainly enjoy listening to these yarns, but this is not history, for one cannot judge whether these stories of mythical times are true. Rather, he will begin his account in historical times with the reign of Croesus of Lydia, the first man whom he knows to have wronged the Greeks without provocation – or so he says. In fact, in telling us about Croesus, he is going to tell us about Croesus's ancestor Gyges, who usurped the throne after his master Candaules had ordered him to look upon the queen naked. It is a compelling story that offers one point of departure for the connection between *The Histories* and *The English Patient*, for Almásy becomes fatally enamoured of the wife of a fellow map-maker when she reads the Gyges story to the assembled company around a campfire in the desert. We have looked at this story before in so far as it bears on the question of origins; it is worth examining again to see how Herodotus deploys it as a paradigm for much that follows in *The Histories*.

The tale of Candaules, Gyges, and the unnamed queen is profoundly revealing of both Herodotus's view of history and his conception of Eastern monarchs. As the story opens, Candaules is happily ruling Lydia, enjoying not only the perquisites of monarchy but the privilege of being married to a woman with whom he is utterly infatuated. He cannot get enough of looking at her – or, it seems, of boasting about her looks, forming a peculiar bond with his right-hand man Gyges by pressuring him to gaze upon her himself, and to do it when she is naked. The visual element is heightened here by Candaules' description of the protracted strip-tease his wife performs nightly: there is a chair, he explains, in the royal bedchamber, on which she will lay each article of clothing one by one as she undresses. Gyges, Candaules insists, must perform a most inappropriate act of voyeurism: Candaules will station him behind the bedroom door to do his beholding, and when he has seen the naked queen, he is to slip out unseen as she walks naked from chair to bed with her back to him. We, the audience, cannot help participating in this voyeurism as well, as we ourselves envision the nude queen moving across the room. We wonder how tall she is, how broad in the hips, whether her hair hangs loose or is piled on her head.

The queen, however, sees Gyges as he exits the royal bedchamber, and she reacts with impressive sangfroid. Had something like this perhaps happened before? Did she say to herself, 'All right, that does it. This is the last time he pulls this stunt!'? It is curious that she does not assume that a coup is afoot, does not cry out for assistance. She knows her husband well – better than he knows her. What he has been seeing when relishing her outward beauty was in fact misleading: she is more threat than treasure. Rather than betraying her emotions during the night, she calmly summons Gyges in the morning and explains that he and Candaules have created a situation in which she has been seen naked by two men. One of them has got to go. Given the choice of killing the king or dying himself, Gyges kills Candaules, marries the queen, and founds a new dynasty.

By her gutsy resolve, this nameless queen has not only preserved her honour (now only one man alive has seen her naked) and punished her traducer, but has reaffirmed the norms of her society: in Lydia, Herodotus points out, it is considered most shameful to be seen naked, even for a man – something that would have surprised readers in the Greek world, where the glorification of the young male body led to nudity in both athletic competition and artistic representation. Gyges certainly showed his understanding that Candaules' wacky plan violated social norms when he begged the king 'not to make me do this thing that is so contrary to custom'. People, he pointed out, can benefit from the long-standing repository of basic truths that include the central tenet that 'each person should look at what is his own'. Things do not turn out well for Candaules, who has set this memorable chain of events in motion, but the queen assures the stability of Lydia, which is likely to fare much better under Gyges than under Candaules, the plaything of his own ungovernable *eros*, and she and Gyges found a dynasty that endures for generations.

Herodotus places this vignette early in *The Histories*, for it has much to tell us – about the dangers of crossing boundaries, of course, as Xerxes does when he bridges the Hellespont, about the risky proclivities of autocrats, about the role of women as actors on the human stage, and about the contingent nature of history: Gyges would never have become king of Lydia had Candaules not had a screw loose, and had not Gyges become king, his descendant Croesus would never have ruled or undertaken to war with Cyrus – by crossing the Halys.

Autocrats, we learn, mistreat women. From this, dramatic consequences flow. When Cyrus and his mad son Cambyses have both died and subsequent usurpers have been dispatched, three prominent Persians hold a debate as to what sort of government they should set up. Some Greeks, Herodotus says, are not convinced of the authenticity of this discussion, but it did, he insists, really take place. Otanes, who speaks first, advocates democracy, which, he maintains, has the fairest name of all – *isonomie*, 'equality before the law'. Not only that; he attacks monarchy on the grounds that a man who rules alone subverts a country's long-established traditions, forces women against their will, and puts men to death without trial. All these elements are present in the Candaules/unnamed queen/Gyges triangle: Candaules violates custom by forcing his wife to be seen naked, and the reluctant assassin Gyges, to save his life, puts Candaules to death without trial. (Otanes, of course, does not persuade the others, for, as we know, monarchy persisted in Persia.)

The Histories is full of monarchs who abuse women – and with Greek autocrats who do so, men whose behaviour Herodotus often portrays as paralleling that of barbarian despots. Frightened by a dream, the Median ruler Astyages plots to murder his daughter's baby son at birth, although the infant escapes death and grows up to become Cyrus, founder of the Persian Empire. Cyrus's son Cambyses, who has married two of his sisters in violation of Persian custom, kills one of them in a rage when she soulfully ponders how vulnerable he has made himself by murdering the brother who might have stood by him in danger. The Corinthian ruler Periander not only murders his wife Melissa but has sex with her dead body. Asiatics in groups exhibit alarming behaviour as well: Persian soldiers gang-rape some Greek women to death.

The failure of Eastern rulers to behave in an appropriately self-protective way (as Candaules plainly did not) interested Herodotus a good deal and offered him a window into the character of the failed bogeyman of the Greeks, Xerxes himself. For in fact, two parallel treatments of the topos bracket *The Histories*: the imprudence of Candaules and the imprudence of the Persian king. Xerxes, it turns out, has no more discretion in matters of *eros* than Candaules. His lack of common sense manifests itself somewhat differently: incongruously, he seeks to seduce the wife of his cherished brother Masistes, and, failing in

69

his efforts, tries again with Masistes' daughter Artaÿnte, whom he marries to his own son to keep her close by. With her, his suit is successful, but this success spells disaster for his family, for in addition to having a brother and a sister-in-law and a niece, he has a wife, Amestris.

In this lurid tale, it is only Amestris who is able to control her destiny. Herodotus makes double use in this *logos* of the motif of the fatal promise. Xerxes is so smitten with his niece/mistress Artaÿnte that he recklessly offers her anything she wants. Now Amestris, Herodotus explains, had woven Xerxes a beautiful shawl, long and colourful, and he often wore it when he went to see Artaÿnte. And it is this very thing Artaÿnte requests from him – for, Herodotus says, 'It was destined that she and her whole family would end badly'. He had said much the same of Candaules. Knowing there would be hell to pay if he were to bestow on her the work of his wife's hands, Xerxes did everything he could to wriggle out of his promise, offering Artaÿnte cities, as much gold as she desired, even the command of an army, but it was useless. All she wanted was the shawl, and once she had it, she made a habit of parading around in it. ('Look what I got from my boyfriend *the king*!') The young Artaÿnte, it seems, is as much of an exhibitionist as Candaules.

Having learned what is going on, Amestris takes advantage of a Persian custom that requires the king, at his birthday party, to grant guests whatever gift they desire: she asks for Masistes' wife. Again, Xerxes protests vigorously, but again he has no choice. Upon gaining possession of the unfortunate woman, Amestris enlists the help of Xerxes' personal guards in cutting off her breasts, nose, ears, lips, and tongue, and packs her off home for Masistes to behold. Livid, Masistes gathers his sons and raises a revolt, but Xerxes' army catches up with them and kills them. Thus, Xerxes has lost a beloved brother, but Amestris has destroyed the family that threatened hers. How happily she and Xerxes continued to live together after this we do not know, but of all the characters in the drama, only she winds up on top: Herodotus's readers would know that Xerxes was murdered some years later in a plot in which the son he cuckolded played a part. Like Candaules' wife, Amestris has been violated by a careless husband – Xerxes would not be the last politician to choose a mistress of dubious discretion – and, like her as well, she makes clear that part of being a good ruler is knowing how to treat one's wife. She is not a very congenial character, but she is bold and determined.

Far from being a mere palace intrigue, then, the first of the tales told in *The Histories* opens the door to wider issues that will play key roles in Herodotus's narrative: the propensity of autocrats (and others in autocratic societies) to mistreat women; the dangers of exhibitionism; the prominence of female agency in history; and the need for men to treat women with dignity.

Throughout, *The Histories* depicts women both acted upon and acting. Since it goes without saying that war will make women its pitiful victims, it is their agency that is most noteworthy. Few of Herodotus's women actually serve in the military, but those who do are memorable: Tomyris, queen of the Massagetae, and Artemisia of Halicarnassus stand out. It is Tomyris who brings down Cyrus, the revered founder of the Persian Empire. That he should die at a woman's hands offers a perfectly rotated image of his birth and upbringing: when his grandfather Astyages had sought to make away with him, it was the lowly Cyno, a shepherd's wife, who took him in and raised him as her own child, restoring balance both to her own family – the infant to whom she had just given birth was stillborn – and to that of the royal house, which, she realized, should not be deprived of its rightful heir. Having reclaimed his heritage and supplanted the scheming Astyages, Cyrus goes on to enjoy an illustrious career – until he meets his match in the form of the Massagetae, who lived east of the Caspian Sea. Several factors, Herodotus says, accounted for his eagerness to attack this people, but the two principal ones were his consistent success in previous campaigns and 'his belief in the miraculous nature of his birth': in other words, had it not been for one woman, Cyno, who saved him (his parents spread the miraculous story that he had been raised by a dog, which is what 'Cyno' meant), Cyrus would never have gone on to attack another one – who destroyed him in what Herodotus called 'the fiercest battle ever fought between non-Greeks'. Tomyris is ruthless and bloodthirsty, and understandably so: she fights not only to defend her land but to avenge her son, who had committed suicide when captured by Cyrus. When she locates Cyrus's head, she shoves it into a wineskin filled with human blood, honouring the promise she had made to him to 'quench his thirst for blood'.

Artemisia of Halicarnassus is a very different story. Herodotus first brings Artemisia on stage when he is listing Xerxes' naval officers: no need, he says, to mention every officer, but one name cannot be omitted, for 'I consider it a wonder that Artemisia, being a woman, should have taken part in the campaign against Greece'. It is no wonder that Herodotus should have been proud of a home-town girl made good, but his interest in her goes beyond pride. In his construction, Artemisia, like Tomyris, serves as a remarkable gender-bender who calls into question conventional sex roles in both Greek and barbarian worlds. Despite having a grown son who could well have commanded her contingent, Herodotus reports, she was moved to go on the expedition by *andreia* – a Greek word denoting both courage and, literally, *manliness*, not characteristics commonly attributed to a woman. This gender peculiarity reappears after the battle of Thermopylae, when Artemisia alone among Xerxes' commanders advises against fighting at Salamis, pointing out that the Persians could easily win by default if they decline to fight the demoralized Greeks. A naval battle is a terrible idea, she says, since – and this is quite an unforgettable observation coming from a female admiral – 'the Greeks are as far superior to your men when it comes to fighting at sea as men are to women'! So far is Artemisia identified with men that she readily buys into their gender stereotyping – at least for rhetorical purposes. (And at least in Herodotus's reconstruction of events.)

Xerxes' other advisers are as unimaginative in guessing at his response as they are in plotting naval strategy; they anticipate that the king will be furious. In fact, he is quite impressed, though, being Xerxes, he cannot believe Artemisia is correct, and he does not take her advice. Herodotus positively thrills to share with us the clever ploy by which Artemisia saved herself: chased by an Athenian ship, in an extraordinary display of quick thinking, she rammed another ship fighting on the Persian side – and sent it straight to the bottom. The Athenian captain assumed she must be either Greek or a deserter from the Persian cause and gave up his pursuit. Xerxes, thinking Artemisia must have sunk a Greek ship (and holding up his end of the discourse on gender), exclaimed 'My men have turned into women and my women into men!'

Artemisia does not, in the end, affect the course of history; her shipboard heroics are not sufficient to prevent a Greek victory. Other women, however, are portrayed as playing significant roles in shaping events. Candaules' wife causes a switch in dynasties in Lydia but also lays the foundation for Croesus's overthrow in the fifth generation as divine retribution for the crime to which she incited Gyges; the slave Cyno rescues and raises Cyrus, and the queen Tomyris brings about his death. Darius no doubt had many motives for invading Greece, the Ionian rebellion among them, but Herodotus's account highlights the chain of events that began with an abscess on the breast of the king's wife Atossa: endlessly grateful to the Greek doctor Democedes who cures her, she accedes to his request that she urge Darius to march on Greece, and her appeal is successful.

A Greek coda: because of the greater prominence of women in public life outside Greece, Herodotus devotes somewhat more space to 'barbarian' than to Greek women, but Greek females play key roles in *The Histories* as well. We are led to believe that the Ionians' rebellion from Persia might have succeeded had Gorgo, the little daughter of the Spartan king Cleomenes, not cautioned her father against taking money from the agitator Aristagoras. Non-Greek patterns have Greek parallels. Although Herodotus associates brutality in Greece primarily with autocratic rulers, he also reproduces the pattern of male action and female re-action among more humble Greek characters. The women of Miletus, he recounts, passed down to their female descendants a law forbidding them to dine with their husbands or to address them by name, and he offers the following explanation: these women had been forced into marriage by Greeks who had murdered their fathers, husbands, and sons. Persian brutality is more common than Greek, but the Persians have no monopoly on cruelty.

The tale of the Milesian women evokes the Amazons, who, as we have seen, also passed their culture on to their children. Lemnos is a different story. There, women also attempted to do this, but their efforts resulted in their deaths and those of their children. Herodotus tells how when the Pelasgians had seized some Athenian women and forced them into concubinage on the island of Lemnos, the women at first fell into the pattern of preserving their culture, teaching not only their daughters but their sons to 'conduct themselves like Athenians and speak Attic Greek'. In time, though, these children began to lord it over the offspring of the Pelasgian women, leading the Pelasgians to worry about what would happen when they grew up. Consequently, the Pelasgians decided to kill the children they had fathered on the Athenian women – and to murder the mothers as well.

To this episode, 'along with the earlier one when the women of Lemnos murdered their husbands', Herodotus ascribes the Greek habit of referring to a particularly heinous crime as a 'Lemnian deed'. The emphasis is striking here: the ancient myth of the Lemnian women's murder of their husbands appears in a throwaway line, while the historical account of men's appalling murder of their concubines and children is highlighted as the cause of the common expression. Yes, women in *The Histories* do dreadful things, but no worse than men, and often in response to male cruelty. They act, re-act, and are acted upon. They can kill, but they can also nurture. When they do kill, Herodotus offers important context. So when after the Battle of Salamis an Athenian, Lycidas, suggests that his fellow citizens consider a Persian offer of peace, the women of Athens go to Lycidas's house and stone his wife and children – but not before the men of Athens have stoned Lycidas himself.

Throughout *The Histories*, Herodotus uses women to illustrate the dangerous proclivities of men, but at the same time women interest him as actors in their own right. This pattern echoes the treatment of non-Greeks in the ethnographies: they are useful to think with because of the way they lead the reader to look at Greek *nomoi* in a new light, but their customs also merit study in and of themselves. Like the different peoples he has studied, the women Herodotus discusses are extraordinarily varied. Herodotus is no essentialist in his approach to women. Ultimately, the broad worldview that declines to regard women as a race apart from men with distinguishing and universal characteristics is one of the key links between *The Histories* and the Homeric epics.

Chapter 6
Herodotus and the divine

The belief that there is 'something out there' beyond the purely human and natural has been persistent throughout history. Despite a dogged minority of sceptics, some closeted, others vociferous, religion has been pretty much of a cultural universal across time and place. Faith in – or fear of – extra-human forces and their power to shape events seems to be pervasive, and a wide network of systems has been designed to gain access to their thoughts and wishes by prayer and/or through the interpretation of such things as omens, dreams, and oracles.

To consider oracles alone: Egyptians established an oracle at Per-Wadjet even before the establishment of the Egyptian state late in the 4th millennium BC; in Herodotus's day, this site was known as Buto, and its oracle was still much revered. Chinese living under the Shang dynasty sought guidance from 'oracle bones'. The Mexica founded Tenochtitlan at the site of what is now Mexico City on the basis of an oracle. In the Himalayan region, oracles continue to play an important role in governmental decision-making and also provide intelligence; the Dalai Lama often consults the state oracle of Tibet, the Nechung Oracle. Some brave souls even petition a new kind of oracle, subjecting themselves to genetic testing that will inform them not only how long they can expect to live but which malady is likely to get them in the end.

Much of *The Histories* turns on the importance of digesting and analysing oracular pronouncements with humility and caution. Not surprisingly, Herodotus uses the way people in his *Histories* respond to divine signs to demonstrate both the character of specific individuals and human nature more broadly – and to say something about what does, and does not, determine the course of history.

Consider Croesus. Alarmed by the growing power of Cyrus, he sends emissaries to a wide variety of oracles throughout Greece as well as to the oracle of Ammon in Libya, testing them to find out which one knew what he was doing on the hundredth day from when his men had set out. When the oracle of Apollo at Delphi hits the nail on the head – he was, of all things, boiling lamb and tortoise meat in a bronze pot – he determines to place his trust in Delphi and makes lavish offerings there. Advised that he should find out which Greek states would make the most powerful allies and that if he went to war with Persia he would destroy a mighty empire, he undertakes an investigation into Greek politics (which affords Herodotus a natural opening for some background on Athens and Sparta). So far, so good; Croesus is behaving like a proper Herodotean inquirer. But in his eagerness to defeat Cyrus, he has neglected to ask which empire he will destroy.

Unwilling to quit while he is (as it might seem) ahead, Croesus goes on to ask whether his reign will last a long time, and the priestess replies that he will be safe until a mule becomes king of Persia. There is much irony in Herodotus's use of prophecies. The audience knows that Lydia would fall to Cyrus, but Croesus does not, and, unacquainted with *Macbeth*, he does not realize that he is being offered false security. Like the Scottish king who takes satisfaction in the prophecy that none of woman born shall harm him, Croesus is delighted by the priestess's response, for how could a mule rule an empire? But just as Macbeth will be undone by Macduff, who was 'from his mother's womb untimely ripp'd',

Croesus is defeated by Cyrus, a half-Mede and half-Persian 'mule'. The folk motif of the 'trick prophecy' makes a hash of Croesus's life and kingdom. For all his comprehensive research, his two lapses from due diligence – checking on which empire will be destroyed, and exploring the possibility that the mule in question is a metaphoric one – prove his undoing.

There is more. The priestess had warned Croesus's ancestor the regicide Gyges that his dynasty would last only through the fifth generation. By having dropped this subject, Herodotus has cleverly arranged for his readers to forget it – just as Croesus had forgotten it. But the king's ultimate fall is doubly determined: Croesus has been careless in his interpretation of the oracle, but he was also the victim of an inexorable fate. It is no coincidence that *The Histories* was composed during the heyday of Greek tragedy in which fate and free will danced around one another with catastrophic results – and which were still more laden with irony than Herodotus's text.

Key figures in the Persian War battles are also revealed to us by the way they respond to oracles. It was because of an oracle proclaiming that a Greek victory at Thermopylae could be bought only with the death of a Spartan king, Herodotus maintains, that King Leonidas dismissed the bulk of his troops. Thus the campaign is portrayed as a willing sacrifice rather than a defeat in battle, and Leonidas heroized. The Athenian Themistocles, for his part, is portrayed as responding to an oracle not with self-sacrifice but with cleverness and political skill: when the oracle at Delphi prophesies that a wooden wall will help the Athenians, it is Themistocles who manages to turn the debate about the prophecy in favour of taking the wooden wall to mean not the fortified Acropolis but the navy. Themistocles and his persuasive powers guide the sometimes acrimonious negotiations among the Greek states. Ever the tough negotiator, he dredges up oracles (real or invented) prophesying that the Athenians would someday relocate in Italy

Herodotus and the divine

10. This early 5th-century vase shows Croesus on the funeral pyre to
which he has been relegated by his conqueror Cyrus. According to
Herodotus and some other Greek writers, he did not die but was
rescued, whether by Cyrus and Apollo or by Apollo alone

to buttress his threat to withdraw the Athenian fleet if the others refuse to fight at Salamis. When the coalition wavers, his cleverness and daring trick the Persians into attacking just as the Greek contingents are in danger of breaking up and scattering to their homes, and a decisive Greek victory follows.

Herodotus's narrative would not be complete without vain attempts to thwart oracles. Corinth, we learn, was ruled by a particularly narrow oligarchy consisting of one clan, the Bacchiads, who married only amongst themselves. Having found no Bacchiad willing to take his lame daughter, Labda, her father married her off to a certain Eëtion, a man from the village of Petra, but the union produced no children. When the disconsolate Eëtion consulted Delphi about his chances for an heir, he was told that Labda was in fact pregnant with a child who would fall upon the Bacchiads like a millstone and bring justice to Corinth. Their work cut out for them, the Bacchiads set about making away with Labda's baby. The picturesque tale that Herodotus tells – or, rather, places in the mouth of one Sosicles of Corinth – is one of the most memorable in *The Histories*.

Soldiers arrive at Petra, wishing, they say, to pay their respects to the newborn out of affection for Eëtion. In reality, they intend to kill it. The man who first gets hold of the infant was supposed to dash it to the ground, but as *theie tyche* (divine chance) would have it, the baby looks up at his would-be murderer and smiles. And so the soldiers play 'hot potato' with the child, finally handing it back to its mother without having found anyone disposed to kill it.

Afraid to face their Bacchiad masters, the soldiers return for a second try, which fails for a different reason: no fool, Labda has realized their intentions and has hidden the boy in a chest (in Greek, a *kypselos*). Unable to find the praeternaturally quiet baby, the soldiers go away, Labda names her son after the chest, and Cypselus grows up to overthrow the Bacchiad aristocracy and become ruler of Corinth. (How this improbable story got started in Corinth one can only imagine: presumably it was designed to explain Cypselus's odd name.)

Herodotus, then, incorporates the oracles that were so ubiquitous in Greek culture into his narrative for a variety of purposes. Croesus's interaction with Delphi reminds the reader of the power of fate and reveals the king's inability to approach the oracle's pronouncements with the required subtlety; just as he rejected Solon's unwelcome wisdom out of hand, he uncritically accepts news that he wants to hear. First, Croesus had tested the oracle, asking it to guess what he was doing back in Lydia, and it passes; then the oracle tests Croesus, and he fails. The result is the expansion of Cyrus's empire. Leonidas's determination to fulfil the oracle that had forecast his death crystallizes the heroism built into the Spartan character and evokes the heroism of Homer's *Iliad*, just as the battle over his corpse evokes the battle over that of Achilles' companion Patroklos. At the same time, his patriotic, sacrificial orientation makes a deliberate contrast with the strongly personal element that drove Homeric heroes, who sought glory not for their cities but for themselves. Themistocles' ability not only to 'divine' the meaning of the 'wooden wall' oracle but to persuade the hesitant Athenians that he is right highlights not only his character but the contingent nature of history: had the Athenians not been fortunate enough to have a Themistocles among them, they might well have failed to place their hope in the navy, stayed in Athens, and been massacred by the Persians. History, wrote Rear Admiral Samuel Morison, 'is like that, very chancy'. The murderous nature of oligarchy is underlined by the death squad sent by the Bacchiads to make away with Labda's baby, but Labda's maternal resourcefulness parallels that of Cyno, the slave woman who rescued and raised the baby Cyrus to adulthood: once more a woman, faced with male violence, rises to the occasion. Though her child does grow up to overthrow her birth family, at least he is alive to do so.

Herodotus, then, uses religion in the service of his narrative agenda. But what of his own convictions? What role did Herodotus ascribe to the divine in shaping the unfolding of events? The question of Herodotus's religious beliefs has been the object of fairly rabid scholarly debate. Some emphasize Herodotus's scepticism; others consider him a conventional Greek of his day who may have braved the seas to satisfy his curiosity about the human world but who accepted unquestioningly the traditional teachings about the Olympian gods. Somewhere in between are those who see him as, well, somewhere in between.

A good place to jump in might be to point out what Herodotus's sense of the divine is *not*. The squabbling, interfering, anthropomorphic gods of, say, the *Iliad*, where Aphrodite is wounded in the wrist and goes crying to Zeus about it, are entirely missing from *The Histories*. Consider the plague that strikes the Greeks early in the poem. When the Greek commander-in-chief Agamemnon refuses to accept ransom in exchange for a war prize whose father happens to be a priest of Apollo, the priest goes to Apollo and asks him to punish the Greeks. The god agrees:

> Down from the peaks of Olympus he strode, a god with his heart full of anger,
> Down with his bow and his quiver, with arrows that clanged on his shoulders....
> Just like the night was his coming, and then the god sat himself down,
> Apart from the ships, and let fly an arrow.
> Shrill was the twang of the bow made of silver. The mules he attacked first,
> And the swift dogs, but then the men...
> And the fires of the corpses burned thickly.

He has a heart, shoulders, a bow, quiver, arrows! He sits down! This Homeric god is far removed from what we find in Herodotus.

Rarely indeed does Herodotus express belief in a specific Olympian. He is far more prone to speak of 'the divine' as a guiding force in human affairs than to construe the principals in the Persian Wars as fighting on earthly terrain while on high quarrelsome Olympians plot to kill them for their sport. What we find in *The Histories* as a whole is rather a transcendent, non-anthropomorphic force at work. Yes, *ho theos*, 'the deity', is often mentioned, but which one is not generally specified, and Herodotus also speaks of *tyche theie*, divine chance; *to theion*, the divine; and *he pronoie tou theiou*, divine providence. Herodotus was not unique in this orientation; his approach to 'that power out there' is evocative of Xenophanes' claim that 'there is one god, among gods and men the greatest, in no way resembling mortals in body or mind'.

What, then, is the province of the transcendent divine in *The Histories*? For one thing, it works almost (but not quite) as a force of nature to maintain balance. Why are there few lions but seemingly infinite bunnies? Herodotus has an answer: *He pronoie tou theiou* – the forethought of the divine – in its wisdom has made timid and tasty creatures prolific, so that the species may not vanish through predation, whereas cruel, baneful animals produce few young. Hares, for example, are the only animals who can conceive while pregnant, so that a single one may carry in her womb foetuses in varying stages of development, some bald, some furry, some still in the process of formation. (Not true. 'Superfoetation' can in fact happen in hares, but the newborns arrive in the same stage of development.) A lioness, on the other hand, produces only a single cub in a lifetime, since the cub's sharp claws destroy the womb as the foetus moves around before birth. (Again, no. Bad logic too, since by this reasoning lions would have reached extinction long before Herodotus's day!) This kind of balancing also appears with respect to Persian War battles themselves: Herodotus cites the divine as the source of a storm off the island of Euboea that dashed a great number of the Persians' ships against the rocky coast in the dark. This, he says, was done 'by the god' to reduce the Persians' numerical advantage at sea and balance out the huge discrepancy between the Greek and Persian numbers. It is not clear that a specifically Greek divinity is intended here; the goal of the unspecified divine seems to be to achieve a 'fair fight'. Thus Miltiades exhorting the Athenians to strike without delay at Marathon: 'we can win this fight if the gods are impartial' (literally, 'if the gods distribute equal things').

Divinity also acts to punish *hybris* and excess. Herodotus plainly takes satisfaction in recording the gruesome end of the Greek dynast Pheretime, who brought down the wrath of 'the gods' (unnamed) by arrogating to herself a vengeance suitable only to the divine. When her son Arcesilaus, king of Cyrene in North Africa, was killed in the town of Barca, Pheretime impaled those she considered most responsible at intervals all around the city walls. Not content with this act of brutality, she also had their wives' breasts cut off and adorned the walls with them as well. Her end, however, was not a happy one, for immediately afterwards she died a horrible death, her body eaten by worms while she was still alive, 'as if to show people that vengeance in excess occasions the gods' displeasure'.

The divine can warn of trouble to come, but not always in a way that makes it possible for the warned to avoid what is in store for them. People generally receive a sign, Herodotus says, of evils ahead, such as the signs given to the people of Chios portending their defeat at the hands of Histiaeus during the Ionian rebellion: of 100 youths whom the Chians had sent to Delphi, only two returned, the other 98 having been killed by a plague; and around the same time, while 120 boys were studying their letters in school, the roof fell in and killed all but one. These warning signs 'the god' had shown them. The divine knows what is ahead, and humans are not always in control of their fate.

Specific gods do intervene when their sanctuaries are involved. Vengeance is mine, says Poseidon when his sanctuary has been violated. While the Persians are besieging Potidaea in northern Greece, Herodotus writes, an exceptionally low tide inspired the Persians to wade through the water. When they were not yet halfway across:

They were caught by the flood that followed which was of corresponding height – in fact, according to the people in the region, higher than it had been previously, although high tides are not unusual there. The men who could not swim drowned, and those who could swim were killed by the Potidaeans, who came after them in boats. The Potidaeans ascribe this excessive tide and the Persians' disaster to the fact that the men who died were the same ones who had previously desecrated the shrine of Poseidon and the statue of him that stands right outside the town.

And not only the Potidaeans believed this: 'Personally', Herodotus writes, 'I think their explanation is the true one.'

In the end, the Greek victory that shaped the future course of history came down to a face-off between the autocratic Xerxes, a man out of touch with realities who consistently rejected good advice and would not be persuaded, and Themistocles, who, being a citizen of a democracy, excelled at persuasion and consistently gave good advice. Did Herodotus not, then, believe that the divine played a role in the outcome of the war?

Perhaps the best way to approach this question is to consider two passages, one from a speech by Themistocles to his fellow Athenians and another in which the historian speaks in his own voice. First, Themistocles:

> It is not we who performed this exploit, but rather the gods and the heroes, who begrudged that one man – and a wicked, impious one at that – should rule over both Asia and Europe.

Next, Herodotus. I find myself compelled, he says, to express an opinion that I know will not be well received (presumably because of the unpopularity of the Athenian empire at the time he was writing). If the Athenians had not stood fast, Greece would have been lost. Without the Athenians, no Greek confederacy could have held together and defeated Xerxes. However many fortifications the Spartans had constructed across the Isthmus, their allies would have deserted them and they would have been left to die fighting. Alternatively, the spectacle of the rest of Greece submitting to Xerxes might have driven them to come to terms with the Persians. After going on in this vein for nearly a paragraph, he concludes:

> One would surely be right to say that Greece was saved by the Athenians.... It was the Athenians who, after the gods, drove back the Persian king.

Themistocles seeks to ingratiate himself with the Athenians by professions of piety, casting Xerxes' defeat as divine punishment for his overreaching *hybris* and ascribing the Greek victories not only to the gods but to the demigods the Greeks worshipped as well, the so-called 'heroes'. Herodotus, by contrast, buries his almost off-hand reference to the gods in a detailed hard-headed analysis of the campaign. In the end, the Athenians are heroic at Marathon, the Spartans at Thermopylae, Themistocles' bag of tricks prevails at Salamis, and an all-out effort at Plataea and Mycale puts an end to Persian ambitions once and for all. Indubitably, gods are present in *The Histories*, but it is the human dimension to which Herodotus accords pride of place.

And yet. Herodotus lived at a time of tremendous intellectual ferment in Greece, when religious belief ranged from unquestioning piety to scoffing scepticism, and he made it his mission to create an intellectual history of his times that would incorporate the *logoi* that were characteristic of the different cultures under consideration: the general plan of his work, he says, is 'to record the traditions of the various peoples just as they were told to me' – adding that while he is bound to record what has been said, he is certainly not compelled to believe it. It would thus be peculiar if his text made no mention of religious epiphanies as they were recounted by 'eyewitnesses'.

The runner Pheidippides, dispatched to Sparta by the
Athenians at Marathon, reported seeing the woodland god Pan,
who complained of the Athenians' inattention to him; after the
war, believing Pheidippides' story, the Athenians built the god a
shrine and held annual races and sacrifices in his honour.
(Later on in Greek history, soldiers in particular took care to
worship Pan, as he was believed to strike sudden terror in
armies – hence our word 'panic'.) A gigantic phantom hoplite
with a beard that overshadowed his shield was said to have
passed by the Greek soldier Epizelus during the battle itself,
blinding him for life. During the invasion of Xerxes, when
thunder and crashing rocks had driven the terrified Persians
from Delphi, those who escaped with their lives told a
miraculous story:

> They saw, so they said, two gigantic hoplites – taller than any man –
> pursuing them and cutting them down. According to the Delphians,
> these figures were Phylacus and Autonous, local heroes who have
> sacred plots of enclosed ground near the temple.

Can we conclude, then, that Herodotus incorporates these *logoi*
simply to give the reader some sense of the experience of battle,
the mindset of the Greek soldier? Not so fast. For the truth is that
Herodotus reports in his own name the material that surrounds
the survivors' tale. The sacred weapons of the god, he says,
inexplicably moved from their customary place within the shrine,
and when the Persians reached the shrine of Athene Pronaea
(Athena in Front of the Temple),

> even greater portents happened to them than the one I just
> reported. It is miraculous enough that weapons of war should move
> of their own accord and turn up on the ground outside the shrine;
> but what transpired next is surely one of the most amazing things
> ever known: just as the Persians came to the shrine of Athene
> Pronaea, thunderbolts fell on them from the sky, and two pinnacles
> of rock, torn from Parnassus, came crashing down among them

with great noise, killing a large number, while at the same time a
battle-cry was heard from inside the shrine....The rocks that
fell from Parnassus were still there in my time.

While Herodotus does not explicitly ascribe these amazing events
to a god – Apollo (because of Delphi), or Athena (because of the
shrine) – we are still left with the impression of a man in awe of
the divine, and we would do well to avoid interning him squarely
in the sceptic camp with no chance of escape.

Chapter 7
Herodotus as storyteller

Herodotus grew up in a world of stories. The Big One – the one that qualified in his day as The Greatest Story Ever Told – was the story of the Trojan War and its aftermath, recounted in the *Iliad* and the *Odyssey* as well as other poems that have not survived. Even the Homeric epics, though, were made up of units like the description of Achilles' shield in the *Iliad* or the Cyclops episode in the *Odyssey*. Herodotus made it his mission to recount The Second Greatest Story Ever Told, and it too was made up of smaller units, self-contained tales that had once enjoyed lives of their own, although not necessarily in the form in which they appear once Herodotus has had his way with them and stretched them to fit his screen. Some of these are frankly digressions. My account, says Herodotus, has always sought out supplementary material: Michael Ondaatje, commenting on this line in *The English Patient*, writes that what we find in Herodotus are 'cul-de-sacs within the sweep of history'. Most, however, are in one way or another microcosms of *The Histories* as a whole and offer guideposts as to how to read the larger text. Slowing down the pace of our journey, these *logoi* enable us to pause and zoom in on one corner of Herodotus's world before resuming our forward march with an enhanced understanding of the big picture and how we might approach Herodotus's account of it.

Precisely because Herodotus does not set forth one over-arching theory of history, he is at pains to make use of his many *logoi* to elucidate the several themes he considers important both in human events and in the examination of them. The awe-inspiring but challenging presence of wonders in the world; the difficulty of obtaining certain knowledge and of communicating it; the use of physical evidence in reconstructing the past; the central nexus of balance, reciprocity, equilibrium, and retribution; the reversal of fortune – these are just some of the themes that appear in Herodotean *logoi*.

The story of Arion, which appears early in the text, was in no way required by what we might call the 'plot' of *The Histories*. Rather, it should be viewed as programmatic of how we might read Herodotus's text. Having left the court of Periander at Corinth, where he had been living, the poet/singer Arion earned a great deal of money in Italy and Sicily. Wanting to return home to Corinth, he hired a crew of Corinthian sailors – who decided to throw him overboard and seize his money for themselves. Arion offered them money in exchange for his life, but the sailors turned him down (thus showing that they had no sense of balance or reciprocity at all) and, rather like Candaules' wife addressing the hapless Gyges, gave him a choice that was no choice, telling him to either kill himself, if he wanted to be buried on land, or jump overboard. Arion then asked permission to perform on the deck in his full ceremonial singing costume, promising to make away with himself right afterwards:

> Pleased at the prospect of hearing a song from the most famous singer in the world, the sailors all pulled back from the stern and assembled amidships. Arion put on his full ceremonial costume, took up his cithara, and, standing on the afterdeck, played and sang 'The Falsetto Song'. Then he leapt into the sea, just as he was, costume and all.

Most unexpectedly, a dolphin materializes and carries Arion on its back to land, and the singer makes his way, still in his singing costume – rather wet and heavy, we must imagine – to the court of

Periander. Understandably sceptical of Arion's tale of the 'dolphin *ex machina*', Periander keeps the poet under guard until the Corinthian sailors appear. Upon interrogation, they insist that they had left Arion safe and sound in south Italy, but they are immediately refuted by Arion, who suddenly appears before them – still (again?) wearing his singing costume. The sailors' deceit is revealed and further denial is useless. This, Herodotus says, is the story as the Corinthians and Lesbians tell it, and he adds as further evidence the existence in his own day of a small bronze figure of a man on a dolphin at the very place where Arion came ashore, purportedly an offering from the singer himself.

Of the many elements at work in this story, one might cite several: the use of Arion's costume, alternately dry and wet and sometimes no doubt quite uncomfortable but always present, to add a strong visual and even tactile component to the tale; the use of an object as confirmation of oral tradition; the element of wonder; the element of self-possession in the face of death; and the element of sceptical inquiry. The good fortune of Arion is indeed a wonder, and wonders were of enormous importance to Herodotus. The programmatic first sentence of *The Histories* announced his intention to memorialize *erga* (deeds, works, things) both *megala* and *thomasta*, great and wondrous, of Greeks and non-Greeks alike; he describes what happened with Arion as an especially great wonder – a *thoma megiston* – that happened in Periander's reign. Wonders abound in *The Histories*. It strikes Herodotus as a wonder that Artemisia, a woman, should have commanded a ship in the war. He ascribes his outsize treatment of Egypt to the exceptionally large number of wonders to be found there, from the upside-down river to the extraordinary architectural marvels. The entire city of Babylon is a wonder, as are the collapsible boats that ply the Euphrates.

Arion's performance followed by his fully clothed leap, moreover, is an act of extraordinary self-possession under the circumstances. Had he intended to swim to shore, surely he would have divested himself of his elaborate costume, and his behaviour forecasts other equally remarkable actions in the face of death: the Spartans, for example, combing their hair before facing the Persians at Thermopylae. To them, no convenient animal appeared. And no helicopter.

Look, our narrator seems to be saying – and very early in his narrative, too – the world is full of wonders, and I will put them before you. You may pause to admire the heroism of a great artist; you may also, if you wish, choose to throw out the whole tale as just too improbable. But you will do so at your peril. And then there is the scepticism of Periander. Judicious caution or excessive mistrust? In the end, Arion is vindicated and Periander's doubts are shown to be misplaced, yet reserving judgement is key to Herodotus's project: Herodotus, too, remains sceptical in the absence of evidence, and through this fishy tale he advises us to follow suit. We are even free to read *The Histories* itself with scepticism and to maintain the same dialogue with its narrator as he does with his sources.

Just as Periander's struggle to obtain certain knowledge about Arion's suspicious story mimics our own task in assessing evidence, other *logoi* underline the difficulty of communicating the knowledge one does have, another challenge in the historian's project. A text which itself has many encoded messages, *The Histories* includes several stories of messages that get by, so to speak, under the radar. Histiaeus, wanting to get a subversive message to Aristagoras but knowing the roads were guarded, shaved the head of a slave, tattooed the message on his scalp, and waited for hair to grow again. He then sent the slave to Aristagoras with instructions to tell Aristagoras to shave his head. When Aristagoras did so, he found a message encouraging him to revolt from the Persian Empire. To discourage the Spartans from restoring Hippias as tyrant of Athens, Sosicles of Corinth narrates a long story about tyranny (the one that included the anecdote about Labda and the corn-bin). Sosicles' tale includes the following memorable anecdote about Periander of Corinth and his contemporary Thrasybulus, tyrant of Miletus. Shortly after succeeding his father as tyrant of Corinth in the 6th century, Periander sent a messenger to Thrasybulus for advice in governing. Thrasybulus said nothing. Rather, he ambled through a cornfield with the man, continually cutting off and throwing away all the tallest and finest ears of wheat. The messenger was mystified and, on returning to Corinth, assured Periander that Thrasybulus was mad; but when he heard what Thrasybulus had done, Periander understood that Thrasybulus was recommending that he kill everyone in Corinth who stood out in excellence from the rest, and this was precisely the strategy he adopted. To this we might add the case of the Persian Artabazus and the Greek traitor Timoxenus, who communicated by wrapping notes around arrows, covering them with feathers, and shooting them to a predetermined place – a plan that turned sour when one of Artabazus's shots hit a Greek in the shoulder and everyone gathered around to help pull out the arrow. . . .

Herodotus loved not only storytelling but storytelling bedecked with superlatives, and he takes great pleasure in recording something that was 'the most X that ever happened', or at least 'the most X of which we know'; thence the obvious relish that attended on the gruesome story of Hermotimus and Panionius – a story that also illustrates one of the fundamental principles that Herodotus sees operating in the universe. It was Hermotimus, Herodotus tells us (with obvious satisfaction), who of all the men we know exacted the greatest retribution for a wrong done to him. As a prisoner of war, Hermotimus had been bought by one Panionius, who, Herodotus says, 'made a living in the unholiest way possible', castrating good-loooking boys and selling them. (Herodotus has Themistocles use the same word, *anosios*, unholy, to describe Xerxes' godless attempt to rule both Asia and Europe.) Now Hermotimus was one of Panionius's victims, but things did not go as badly for him as they did for some of the others, for he wound up as Xerxes' most valued eunuch. Many years later, he

chanced to meet Panionius, and, thanking him for the many
benefits that had come his way as a result of his castration, he
encouraged Panionius to move close to him with his entire family.
Bizarrely (for, of course, the story would not work otherwise),
Panionius falls for this ruse. Once he has him in his clutches,
Hermotimus denounces Panionius for his foul deeds and compels
him to castrate his sons – and the sons to then castrate Panionius.
'And this', Herodotus concludes, 'is how Retribution and
Hermotimus caught up with Panionius'.

The Spartan king Cleomenes experienced retribution as well. He
went crazy, Herodotus reports, and was put in the stocks by his
relatives. Bullying his jailer into giving him a knife, he began to
mutilate himself, starting with the shins and moving up to the
thighs and hips, finally dying when he had begun cutting his
stomach into strips. There were several theories current about just
what transgression had brought him down; his own opinion,
Herodotus says, is that Cleomenes came to grief as retribution for
having bribed the priestess at Delphi to help him depose his rival
king Demaratus (the same man who subsequently served as
Xerxes' adviser). What goes around comes around.

The word Herodotus uses to describe the retribution that
overtook both Panionius and Cleomenes is *tisis*, a key Greek
concept that focuses on the maintenance of balance in the world.
As the pre-Socratic Anaximander put it, 'Everything pays *tisis* as
things unfold in time'. *The Histories* shows us how *tisis*
encompasses both what Xerxes wants from the Athenians – first
payback for his father's defeat at Marathon and later punishment
for the Persians' losses at Artemisium – but also the way in which
balance is maintained in the animal world: thus the population of
vipers is kept down by the fact that the female bites through the
male's neck at the moment of ejaculation, killing him, but the
young thus created exact *tisis* from the mother, eating their way
through her womb. Herodotus's concept of *tisis* is much more
sophisticated than Xerxes'; for Herodotus, compensatory *tisis*

extends as far as maintaining the balance of nature, minimizing the number of predators and maximizing the number of preyed-upon (rabbits, birds, and us).

It is a similar concern for equilibrium that motivates Herodotus's enthusiasm for the Babylonian marriage auction and draws him to note that whereas Greece has by far the best climate, the remotest parts of the world sport what is rarest, loveliest, and in some cases biggest. (Note again the superlatives.) Large, fierce animals are most likely to be found at the ends of the earth. Gold is found in great quantities in both India to the east and Ethiopia to the south. Arabia is so rich in spices that the entire country is an olfactory paradise. But Greece, the centre of Herodotus's world both literally and figuratively, has the best climate; it is a place in which one could actually live and the reference point for the wider world.

More than anything else in Herodotus's narrative, it is the disturbance of equilibrium that sets in motion the chain of events that we call history. These disturbances often take the form of transgressions of one kind or another. Candaules violates *nomos* first in becoming infatuated with his own wife, a disruptive passion for a king even within the marital bond, and second in placing his naked wife before Gyges, and Gyges violates *nomos* in both watching the queen and killing the king. Gyges' descendant Croesus longs for more than is his allotted portion, crosses the Halys River to fight Cyrus, and loses his empire; Cyrus in turn, riding the crest of many victories and believing himself invincible, pushes the envelope by crossing the Araxes to fight the fierce Massagetae and is killed by Queen Tomyris. Xerxes snickers at alien (Greek) *nomoi*, desires to violate the natural diversity of cultures, and formulates a plan whereby he and his army shall make the Persian Empire coterminous with the entire world, its boundaries being the sky of Zeus himself, 'so that the sun will not look down upon any land beyond our borders': with your help, he tells his 'advisers' (in whose advice he has minimal interest),

'I shall pass through Europe from end to end and make all the lands a single land'. To Herodotus, who so cherishes the infinite variety of the multicultural world Xerxes wishes to flatten into uniformity that he devoted a large portion of *The Histories* to ethnography, this is a transgression of the highest order. Herodotus, who sought to break down the great wall of misunderstanding that led the Greeks to dismiss foreign *nomoi* as inferior, who created a hybrid genre that combined hard-headed political analysis with folk tale, nonetheless stood firm in his opposition to the crossing of certain kinds of boundaries – the boundaries that enabled different ethnicities to continue within their own *nomoi* and discouraged actions like the stabbing of Apis or the bridging of the Hellespont. Compare Ondaatje's Almásy: falling in love with the wife of a fellow map-maker as she recites the story of Gyges by the firelight, he finds himself impelled to cross agreed-upon boundaries and enters into a disastrous relationship with her, one that in the end kills all three parties to the triangle. Almásy's love for Katharine, Ondaatje writes, 'wishes to burn down all social rules, all courtesy' – in short, all *nomoi*.

Since the greatest attempt at destabilizing equilibrium in the world of *The Histories* was Persian aggression, it is not surprising that Herodotus includes several *logoi* on the theme of underdogs whose cunning saved them from being overmastered by the more powerful. Herodotus takes particular satisfaction in telling how the Phocians foiled an attempted raid by the Thessalians: anticipating an attack by the notoriously formidable Thessalian cavalry, they dug a deep trench, put large empty jars in it, covered them over lightly with soil and smoothed over the surface. When the confident Thessalians galloped up to the attack, their horses fell through into the jars, breaking their legs. A parallel resourcefulness enabled the Babylonian queen Nitocris to keep the hostile Medes out of her city: she diverted the course of the Euphrates so that the once straight river now twisted so much that it actually passed one village three separate times on three different days, and the arduousness of the resulting trip was successful in discouraging attempts to navigate the winding waterway.

The ingenuity of the Phocians and of Nitocris, however, is as nothing to the ingenuity embodied in the intricate tale of the Egyptian ruler Rhampsinitus and the clever thief. Rhampsinitus, his Egyptian sources told Herodotus, had a stone chamber built to store his great treasure, but his efforts achieved a paradoxical result: the man he engaged to build the chamber placed one stone in such a way that it could easily be removed by his sons after his death. When the builder died, the sons did exactly as they had been instructed and thus little by little siphoned off the king's treasure into their own possession. Seeing his treasure diminishing, the king set a trap and indeed caught one of the brothers. Cut off my head, said the captured brother to his sibling, because if they recognize me, you will be ruined too! And his brother did as he suggested.

Foiled again, the king hung the thief's headless corpse on a wall and charged the guards to seize anyone they saw weeping nearby. Understandably distressed, the mother of the two young men ordered her surviving son to retrieve the body, which he did in the following way: he pretended to spill some wine near the site, which the guards lapped up as he pretended to be angry with them. The guards sought to pacify him, and in time they were all drinking merrily together. The guards finally passed out, enabling the thief to cut down his body and return it to his mother.

We're not done yet. The story goes, Herodotus says – though he assures us that he does not believe it – that Rhampsinitus then set up his daughter as a prostitute, bidding her inquire of each customer about the cleverest trick and greatest crime he had committed – another set of superlatives. (Even in stories for which he conspicuously does not vouch, there is a great deal of inquiring in *The Histories*.) Our thief came to visit the young woman with an arm he had cut off from a man who had recently died, and when she asked him the usual questions, he boasted of cutting off his brother's head when the brother had been caught in the king's trap in the treasury and retrieving his brother's body by getting the guards drunk. When the princess tried to grab him, he gave her the dead man's arm instead of his own and made his escape. Rhampsinitus was so impressed by the thief's ingenuity that he tracked him down and took him for a son-in-law.

This charming folk tale plays into Herodotus's larger themes on several levels: the victory of wiliness and courage over power and status; the restoration of balance that comes with the redistribution of wealth; the reversal of fortune. The king who places so much importance on his wealth is evocative of both Croesus and Xerxes, though of course the infinite variety of Herodotus's text imbues the story with a jollity in which all rejoice at the end (except, of course, for the unfortunate dead brother, of whom we are encouraged to lose sight). Wiliness is key for Herodotus: in the end, it was the cunning of Themistocles, of course, that was pivotal in the Greek victory, enabling a poor nation with few soldiers to defeat the mighty Persian Empire, and scholars have speculated that in his portrayal of Themistocles, Herodotus sought to embody both the intellectual brilliance of Athens and its calculated conversion of the postwar league that it led into its own personal empire.

Chapter 8
Herodotus as historian

She sits on the floor, big and grey and increasingly petulant. For a long time, she stood, but she got tired. Her eyes say it all. No more stories: when are they going to start talking about *me*?

She is the elephant in the room. She is the doubt that Herodotus in fact merits the title of historian which I have so blithely bestowed on him. Does he?

On two occasions in his narrative, Herodotus comments that he only reports what he has been told by his various sources, and he considers himself under no obligation to believe it. This deft move enables him to present his work as not only a political and military history of the Persian Wars, but as a social and intellectual history of the then-known world in which tall tales retailed by his informants as well as dearly held beliefs about local history play a legitimate role. Ondaatje's Almásy expresses some of this when he says, 'We are communal histories, communal books'. In *Running in the Family*, Ondaatje offered a supposed apology for the fictional elements in the book, observing that 'in Sri Lanka, a well-told lie is worth a thousand facts'. Byron had some interesting remarks on so-called lies in *Don Juan*:

> And, after all, what is a lie? 'Tis but
> The truth in masquerade; and I defy
> Historians, heroes, lawyers, priests, to put

11. Since heads of prominent Greeks were rarely sculpted from life, we cannot be confident of the resemblance, but this was purportedly Herodotus of Halicarnassus, our author

A fact without some leaven of a lie.

Do historians really belong on this list?

Herodotus's most severe critics say no. Can't you see, they cry? All these source citations – 'the priests told me', 'the Macedonians say', 'that is the Cretan version...but the Carians disagree', etc. – this pretence of eyewitness evidence: isn't that what someone would say *if he were making it all up*? Herodotus did not travel extensively, they contend; rather, he relied on the reports of others, and when those were lacking, as they usually were, he simply invented. These allegations are of different sorts: some scholars maintain Herodotus was simply lying through his teeth, trying to put one over on his audience, while others argue that he was writing in a well-recognized fictional genre and that his contemporaries had no idea that we moderns would hold even the most plainly folkloric *logoi* in *The Histories* to an evidentiary standard that had not yet been developed. How can we deal with these claims?

Herodotus does say that he travelled extensively. His detailed descriptions of dedications at Delphi in mainland Greece and Miletus in Ionia leave little doubt that he saw them with his own eyes, but he also states explicitly that he travelled as far south as Elephantine at the first cataract of the Nile and as far north as the Black Sea region while investigating the Scythians, as well as to Tyre in Phoenicia. Less explicitly, he certainly wants us to believe that he was in Babylon and at Cyrene, in Libya. Can we be sure that he really travelled quite this widely?

If we're going to be completely honest with ourselves, we have to admit that we can't. In some instances, Herodotus may have obtained information from the occasional transplanted native, previous visitor, or written text, rather than going in person as he suggests – or, in some cases, insists. A fragment from Hecataeus makes clear that he was the source for Herodotus's lamentable description of the hippopotamus – complete with the mane and tail of a horse. Not only hadn't Herodotus seen a hippo; apparently Hecataeus hadn't either! And we must also acknowledge that some of the things he says beggar belief. Two examples present different kinds of challenges. Both the Egyptians and the Arabians, he writes, say that the ibis is greatly revered in Egypt because of the service it does in killing the winged snakes that fly there from Arabia. And not only this: he reports that *he himself saw the flying snakes' skeletons in innumerable quantities.* That is impossible, because there are no winged snakes, nor were there in Herodotus's day. What did he see that he could have mistaken for the skeletons of winged serpents? Not clear, and his detractors have seized on this as palpable evidence of deceit on Herodotus's part. Others claim that the Greek text can be construed to mean not skeletons but 'remains' and that he might have meant locusts, and still others regard it as a mystery not yet solved. Then there is the case of Meles and the lion. Meles, Herodotus tells us, a king of Sardis, was told that the city would never be taken if he carried the lion that his concubine had borne him around its walls. And so he dutifully had the lion carried around the fortifications, except at one spot where he deemed the sheer drop sufficient defence. It was at this steep spot that Cyrus's men later took the city when Croesus was king.

Lion borne by concubine? What an interesting recipe for success: 'Take the lion to which your concubine has given birth and....' This is certainly disquieting, and perhaps more than any other passage in *The Histories*, this casual throwaway line makes us want to visit Herodotus in the Underworld and ask him what was going through his mind when he wrote these words – in his own voice, yet, with none of this 'it is said that...' or 'the people of Sardis claim'. If we did – would he answer with a wink?

Let us play devil's advocate and ask how Herodotus could have known anything at all about his subject matter in so far as it concerned times and places distant from his own world. He understood no language but his own, his native informants may have been ignorant (or mischievous – 'You'll never guess what that Greek chap fell for today'!), and oral tradition is unreliable, particularly after the third generation. Much of what he says seems dubious to us. He vastly overestimates the size of Xerxes' army – 2,317,610 men to start with, then 2,641,610 by the time the king had picked up allies on his way, and finally a grand total of 5,283,220 people, counting the slaves and camp followers and crews of the provision boats and other craft that set forth with the expedition. By Herodotus's reckoning, while the first soldiers were arriving at Thermopylae, the last would have been just setting out from Susa. They drank rivers dry as they marched. Xerxes' army is not only the biggest thing in *The Histories*; it is the thing whose size is most defining of the entire work. As for the famed Marathon charge, experiments conducted at the Pennsylvania State University in the United States suggest that nobody can run a mile in hoplite armour. Regarding Arion, why would both the Corinthians and the Lesbians have made up the same story about the dolphin rescue? Persian names did not all end in –s as Herodotus claimed. Hieroglyphic records make clear that no Apis calf died the year of Cambyses' arrival in Memphis. Herodotus seems to be using the customs of the Scythians to define an opposition between them and the Greeks; should we not then wonder whether what he says about them is true? Surely those gold-digging ants in India strain credibility? The monument dedicated at Delphi after Plataea did not have an inscription on the tripod, as Herodotus says, but rather on the base, and it did not consist of a serpent with three heads, as reported in *The Histories*, but rather of three intertwined snakes with one head each. Yet Herodotus claims great familiarity with the offerings at Delphi: is he really not so familiar with them at all? And certainly, we are going to reserve judgement where the Rhampsinitus *logos* is concerned.

These seeming falsehoods fall into several categories. The inflated numbers of Xerxes' forces may have been a simple mistake – perhaps Herodotus confused the Persian chiliad of 1,000 men with a myriad of 10,000; alternatively, he may have exaggerated to throw the Greek victory more sharply into relief, but he just as well may have lacked a grasp of large numbers. As for the purported mile-long charge of the Athenians at Marathon, it is easy to see how soldiers could have remembered it that way – strenuous tasks often seem more strenuous still in the remembering – and even easier to see how they might have exaggerated for effect in recounting the details of their stunning victory. Concerning Arion, there were cults of dolphin-riders in both

Corinth and Methymna, a large town on Lesbos, as well as in Taenarum, the point on the Peloponnesus where Arion was said to have landed. (Dolphin rescues were later recorded for Christian saints. I will not commit myself as to the historical propensity of dolphins to ferry marine hitchhikers.) That all Persian names ended in –s was a flat-out (and inconsequential) error based on ignorance: Herodotus mistook the Hellenized versions for the originals. Cambyses' unwelcome invasion of Egypt affords ample explanation of why local priests would invent the tale of his stabbing an Apis calf, a thoroughly believable story that Herodotus had no reason to dismiss. Archaeological evidence suggests that Herodotus's account of Scythian burial practices was grounded in fact: excavations of burial mounds have turned up such finds as the dozen horses in full dress regalia found in Kazakhstan in 1999. And not only that; classicist Stephanie West and others have shown that the Scythian 'message' to Darius consisting of the bird, mouse, frog, and arrows turns out to be of a piece with other communications between pre-literate peoples. In 1303, the Mongol Prince Toktai sent his rival Noghai a hoe and arrow, and a handful of earth, tokens that Noghai interpreted as 'If you hide in the earth, I will dig you out. If you rise to the heavens, I will shoot you down. Choose a battlefield.' This seems to have been pretty much what Toktai intended, but misinterpretations are always possible: in 1819, a Russian officer presented the Khan of Khiva with two loaves of sugar, ten pounds of lead, ten pounds of gunpowder, and ten musket-flints. The Khivans inferred that the sugar loaves offered peace and sweet friendship, while the ammunition indicated that if they did not agree to such friendship, the Russians would make war on them. In reality, the Russians intended no such thing: they just thought that this selection of items would make a rather nice gift! Still, the misunderstanding makes clear the historicity of messages such as the one Herodotus ascribes to the Scythians. As for the infamous gold-digging ants, we may be dealing with a simple language problem. In the late 20th century, French ethnologist Michel Peissel and other explorers discovered the coarse-furred rodents known as marmots, about the size and weight of a domestic cat, throwing up gold-bearing soil while digging their burrows in one of the most inaccessible regions of the Himalayas, and the people living there reported that they had in fact been profiting from the marmots' labours for generations. The Persian word for 'marmot' was taken by Herodotus to mean 'mountain ant'. Not such a tall tale after all, perhaps. Regarding the famous serpent column, the Roman emperor Constantine had it moved to Constantinople, where I myself enjoyed autopsy of it in 1993. The heads fell off some two millennia after Herodotus's death, but the snakes' bodies remain intact, and had I not come to the scene knowing otherwise, I would quite possibly have taken them for a single snake.

The story of Rhampsinitus purportedly recounted by Egyptian priests was plainly constructed by piling one folk motif upon another. Significantly, it is at this juncture that Herodotus, who has already distanced himself twice from the story by ascribing it to others, announces that 'Anyone who finds things like this believable can make of these Egyptian tales what he wishes. My job, throughout this account, is merely to record whatever I hear from each of my sources.' Herodotus is certainly covering himself here – perhaps even more than necessary, since plainly his readers will not orient themselves towards this story the same way they will to the victory at Salamis.

In the end, the amount of accurate information in *The Histories* is amazing in light of the many obstacles that stood in the way: vast distances, language barriers, malicious or good-humoured deceptions by local informants. Ongoing archaeological investigations in many parts of the world continue to confirm the truth of much of what we find in Herodotus; the Scythian burials are just the tip of the iceberg. Egyptologists continue to be astounded by how much Herodotus got right. Specialists who can read languages that stumped Herodotus have discovered that the ancient texts confirm his findings more often than they refute them. And some of what Herodotus reports could, if false, have easily enough been refuted by his fellow Greeks. Some of his detractors have zeroed in on his numbering of the Athenian dead at Marathon as 192, no more and no less, maintaining that he invented this precise number to add verisimilitude to the notably small number of men he claims the Athenians lost. But the Athenians knew full well how many men were killed there. Their names were recorded on funeral markers: the inscription commemorating the dead from the one-tenth of the Athenians who belonged to the Erechtheid tribe has now been discovered, and it seems to bear 25 to 30 names, a figure which would confirm total casualties of about 200 for the battle.

And that serpent column at Delphi – easiest thing in the world to check. Everyone went to Delphi. Very risky to put it in if he does not sincerely believe that his description is correct. The most natural explanation by far of his astonishing rate of success is that, by and large, he went where he said he did and thought he had seen what he said he had, although misperception and faulty memory inevitably played a role.

12. **The burial mound covering the Athenian dead at Marathon**

One of the strongest confirmations of both the accuracy of Herodotus's informants and the solidity of his reasoning comes from a curious example in which his logic betrays him, compromised as it was by his limited understanding of the shape of the Earth. Some Phoenicians claiming to have circumnavigated Africa (clockwise, through the Red Sea down the east coast and then up towards the Straits of Gibraltar) reported that they had the Sun on their right hand as they rounded the cape – a thing, Herodotus says, 'which I cannot believe, although someone else may'. He is wrong, of course, but his logic was impeccable: had the Earth really been flat, as he thought, the Phoenicians' tale would have been a tall one indeed.

The Histories is rife, moreover, with examples of Herodotus using his critical faculties to assess the data that have come to him just as a modern historian would do. He is a born sceptic and frequently relegates the so-called data that have been thrown at him to the junk pile. Indeed, he is more critical of some travellers' tales than later authors were: he categorically refuses to believe that the mountains to the north (the Urals?) harbour humans with the feet of goats, although other ancient sources happily located men with horses' feet in the north, as medieval writers did men with the feet of oxen.

Yet, in the last analysis, the issue at hand is not simply to what extent The Histories is factually correct. After all, to paraphrase Herodotus himself, facts which seem now to be accurate may be shown in the future to be inaccurate, and notions which seem wrongheaded today may someday be proven quite on target. Take the matter of the Etruscans. Historians have long been sceptical about Herodotus's claim that this pre-Roman people hailed from Anatolia, but recent DNA evidence uncovered in both humans and cattle suggests that Herodotus was absolutely right. History, as Dutch historian Pieter Geyl has pointed out, is an argument without end. And the argument is not just about facts; what a dreadful prospect. For a historical narrative, a modicum of facts is necessary, but hardly sufficient. A collection of facts does not establish a work as a history – nor does an admixture of fiction vitiate its claim to be one. Ancient historians were artful in the presentation of what they considered a higher reality, hence the intrusion into their work of speeches, and even in some cases individuals about whom they could in fact know little, inserted into the text to heighten drama and/or give us a sense of what people would have been thinking and saying. We might even say that they 'Photoshopped' their narratives to make them suit their purposes; how we feel about that may depend on what we think of Photoshopping in general, with its addition of puffy clouds above the apple orchard or its elimination of distracting background behind the images of grandchildren at their piano recitals. What we find among the Greek and Roman historians is more often than not something like the 'docudramas' of modern times, a hybrid form in which minor characters disappear and composite ones are made up in order to draw attention to the underlying dynamics at issue.

Of this genre Herodotus was the inventor. His groundbreaking creation blended painstaking research and charming folk tale, and perhaps we can learn not to be unduly unsettled by this. Who has ever labelled a folk tale a lie? And consider the Scottish journalist Neal Ascherson's comments on the question of where to place Kapuściński's work on the frontier between literature and reportage: 'It's a hard question to answer, not least because there is no such wire barrier (floodlit and dog-patrolled) between the two forms.' Herodotus was said to have been a friend of Sophocles; Kapuściński was a friend of Gabriel García Márquez. Herodotus would have regarded the more fanciful tales in *The Histories* as enrichment of his central *logos* about the Persian Wars rather than grounds for undercutting his integrity as a historian. Some of these stories had something important to tell us about the human condition, others about the richness of our common imagination. Comments from fellow Greeks show that they considered his narrative to be a historical work. Writing in the next century about the difference between poetry and history, Aristotle maintained that Herodotus's narrative would have been a history even if it were turned into verse, the clearest recognition we could hope for that his fellow Greeks classified his work as...history. The author of the treatise *On the Sublime*, writing when Greece was under Roman domination, described him as 'the most Homeric of historians'.

That is a great compliment, but more is to be said, for Herodotus's principles of inclusion were very different from those of an epic poet. Intellectual historian Morton White has assembled seven principles of inclusion in historical writing:

1) the principle of aestheticism: what should be preferred is what is most interesting or aesthetically pleasing;
2) the principle of abnormalism, what is most unusual or bizarre;
3) the principle of moralism, what is morally instructive;
4) the principle of pragmatism, what is useful in relation to present problems;
5) the principle of essentialism, what constitutes the 'main tendencies' or 'essential nature' of the subject;
6) the principle of encyclopaedism, what comes closest to expressing the whole truth about it;
7) the principle of modified encyclopaedism, what best organizes all the available evidence pertaining to the subject.

Gracious! Herodotus was plainly a man of enormous energy. For he checks out on every single count. The enchanting stories (1); the fantastic customs and wonders worth recording (2); the consequences of *hybris* and transgression (3); the dangers of imperialism (4); the fragility of prosperity and the concomitant movement towards balance and reciprocity (5); the many threads that go to make up the vast tapestry of history (6); and the weaving of those threads into patterns, themes, and motifs that tell a coherent story (7): all this we find in *The Histories*. And

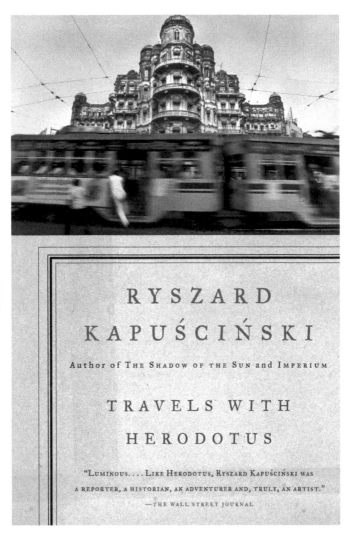

13. In his *Travels with Herodotus*, Ryszard Kapuściński offered a complementary view of war, wonder, and the human condition

more: for there is always the divine hovering in the background. People make good decisions sometimes and bad ones sometimes, but their control over their lives is limited. Take the blinding wind and rain that decreased the Persian fleet near Artemisium, a storm that Herodotus attributes to divine will, or the divine force that accounted for the rumour that reached the Greeks of the victory at Plataea just as they were about to engage the Persian forces at Mycale; think of the Persians who drowned at Potidaea as Poseidon exacted retribution for the violation of his sanctuary.

The multifaceted *Histories* attained their avowed goal of memorializing the past – of organizing a vastly diverse body of data into written form so as to guarantee the survival of many endangered oral traditions. And not only that: while Thucydides created the narrowly focused war monograph, Herodotus created the genre of the comprehensive social and intellectual history. His work has stood the test of time. *The Histories* was in heavy demand during the Renaissance: 44 editions and translations of *The Histories* appeared in Europe between 1450 and 1700. Though his ethnographies raised eyebrows both in his lifetime and for many centuries after his death, the discoveries of explorers in the new world during the 16th century revolutionized the way Europeans looked at Herodotus's work by making them recognize the vast multiplicity of cultures in the world.

Herodotus lives on, of course, in popular culture – in the race named after the Athenian Pheidippides' run to Sparta, for example, seeking assistance at Marathon. The very name of Marathon has even contributed its last syllable to the word 'telethon' made up to designate the sustained hours of irksome television broadcasting that interrupt regular programming to raise money for a worthy cause. Although the Hotel Herodotus closed in the historian's home town in the 1990s, there is still a street named after him in the fashionable Kolonaki district in Athens. Sales of *The Histories* spiked after Anthony Minghella's Oscar-winning film of *The English Patient* hit the theatres, to jump again after the Thermopylae-themed film *300* made from Frank Miller's graphic novel; historical novels like Steven Pressfield's *Gates of Fire* have also done their share to keep the flame alive. The significance of Herodotus's work, however, goes way beyond a high visibility in mass culture that may well prove ephemeral. For even with all his tall tales and exaggerated numbers, Herodotus gave birth to history. To play at the game of famous firsts so dear to his own heart, we may say that it was Herodotus who first, in the words of Hellenist Christian Meier, 'provided historical answers to historical questions'.

It is profoundly ironic that despite the interest in 'barbarian' civilizations he sought to spark in his fellow Greeks, it should ultimately have been Herodotus who breathed life into the idea of the West: putting together his (not altogether neat) oppositions between East and West with the immortality he guaranteed for those who died fighting off the Persians, he, beyond all other writers, bequeathed to subsequent generations the notion of 'Western civilization', a civilization characterized by freedom in government, in speech, in thought. Today, of course, the notion that this thing we call 'Western' is the gold standard of civilizations is giving way in many quarters to a broader view of the human community, one in which no one civilization has a monopoly on civic virtues and excellence in intellect and the arts. Herodotus would have been fascinated. In other quarters, what seems significant about our age is a new clash of cultures that once again is pitting East versus West. Herodotus would have been fascinated by that too. If he were only here, he might pick up his stylus and get started on *The Histories*, volume 2.

Further reading

The Oxford Classical Dictionary, 3rd edn., edited by Simon Hornblower and Antony Spawforth (Oxford and New York: Oxford University Press, 2003) provides an excellent single-volume encyclopaedia of the classical world.

Herodotus's work can be read in many good English translations. The Histories also appears in the Loeb Classical Library series in four volumes, with Greek text on the left and English translation by A. D. Godley on the right (Cambridge, MA, and London, 1920–5).

An enormous amount has been written on Herodotus in English alone. I list here some books and articles that I think would deepen readers' understanding of Herodotus and his times. Inevitably, some of these works contain a bit of Greek, sometimes in Greek font and sometimes transliterated, but they can nonetheless be read with profit by the Greekless reader.

Collections of essays on Herodotus and his age

Egbert J. Bakker, Irene J. F. De Jong, and Hans Van Wees, Brill's Companion to Herodotus (Leiden and Boston: Brill, 2002).
Deborah Boedeker (ed.), 'Herodotus and the Invention of History', Arethusa, 20, nos. 1–2 (1987).
Carolyn Dewald and John Marincola (eds.), The Cambridge Companion to Herodotus (Cambridge: Cambridge University Press, 2006).

Nino Luraghi (ed.), *The Historian's Craft in the Age of Herodotus* (Oxford and New York: Oxford University Press, 2001).

Outstanding books and articles

Wolfgang Aly, *Volksmärchen, Sage und Novelle bei Herodot und seinen Zeitgenossen* (Göttingen: Vandenhoeck and Ruprecht, reprint 1969).

W. M. Bloomer, 'The Superlative *Nomoi* of Herodotus's *Histories*', *Classical Antiquity*, 12 (1993): 30–50.

Carolyn Dewald, 'Women and Culture in Herodotus' *Histories*', in *Reflections of Women in Antiquity*, ed. Helene P. Foley (New York, London, and Paris: Gordon and Breach Science Publishers, 1981), pp. 91–125.

J. A. S. Evans, *Herodotus, Explorer of the Past: Three Essays* (Princeton, NJ: Princeton University Press, 1991).

Stewart Flory, *The Archaic Smile of Herodotus* (Detroit, MI: Wayne State University Press, 1987).

Charles Fornara, *Herodotus: An Interpretive Essay* (Oxford: Clarendon Press, 1971).

John Gould, *Herodotus* (London: Weidenfeld and Nicolson, 1989).

François Hartog, *The Mirror of Herodotus: The Representation of the Other in the Writing of History*, tr. Janet Lloyd (Berkeley and Los Angeles: University of California Press, 1988).

Simon Hornblower (ed.), *Greek Historiography* (Oxford: Oxford University Press, 1994).

Virginia Hunter, *Past and Process in Herodotus and Thucydides* (Princeton, NJ: Princeton University Press, 1982).

Henry Immerwahr, *Form and Thought in Herodotus* (Cleveland: The Press of Western Reserve University, published for the American Philological Association, Chapel Hill, NC, 1966).

Leslie Kurke, *Coins, Bodies, Games, and Gold: The Politics of Meaning in Archaic Greece* (Princeton, NJ: Princeton University Press, 1999).

Mabel L. Lang, *Herodotean Narrative and Discourse* (Cambridge, MA: Harvard University Press, 1984).

Donald Lateiner, *The Historical Method of Herodotus* (Toronto: University of Toronto Press, 1989).

Richmond Lattimore, 'The Wise Advisor in Herodotus', *Classical Philology*, 34 (1939): 24–39.

John Marincola, *Greek Historians* (Oxford: Oxford University Press, 2001).

Rosaria Vignolo Munson, *Telling Wonders: Ethnographic and Political Discourse in the Work of Herodotus* (Ann Arbor, MI: University of Michigan Press, 2001).

Christopher Pelling, 'East Is East and West Is West – Or Are They? National Stereotypes in Herodotus', http://www.dur.ac.uk/ Classics/histos/1997/pelling.html. (accessed 18 January 2011).

James Redfield, 'Herodotus the Tourist', *Classical Philology*, 80 (1985): 97–118.

M. Rosellini and S. Saïd, 'Usage de femmes et autres nomoi chez les "Sauvages" d'Hérodote. Essai de lecture structurale', *Annali della Scuola Normale Superiore di Pisa, Classe di Lettere e Filosofia*, 3rd series, 8 (1978): 849–1005.

Gordon S. Shrimpton, *History and Memory in Ancient Greece*, with an appendix on Herodotus's sources by G. S. Shrimpton and K. M. Gillis (Montreal and Buffalo, New York: McGill-Queen's University Press, 1997).

Rosalind Thomas, *Herodotus in Context: Ethnography, Science, and the Art of Persuasion* (Cambridge: Cambridge University Press, 2002).

K. H. Waters, *Herodotus the Historian: His Problems, Method, and Originality* (Norman, OK: University of Oklahoma Press, 1985).

Stephanie West, 'The Scythian Ultimatum (Herodotus IV 131–132)', *Journal of Hellenic Studies*, 108 (1988): 207–11.

On the veracity of Herodotus

A great deal has been written on the historical accuracy of Herodotus's writings. The two most combative books are by Fehling (against) and Pritchett (for):

Detlev Fehling, *Herodotus and His 'Sources': Citation, Invention, and Narrative Art*, tr. J. G. Howie (Liverpool: Francis Cairns, 1988).

W. Kendrick Pritchett, *The Liar School of Herodotos* (Amsterdam: J. C. Gieben, 1993).

On Persia and the Persian Wars

Richard Billows, *Marathon: The Battle that Changed Western Civilization* (New York: Overlook Press, 2010).

A. R. Burn, *Persia and the Greeks: The Defence of the West, c. 546–478 BC*, 2nd edn., with a postscript by D. M. Lewis (Stanford, CA: Stanford University Press, 1984).

Paul Cartledge, *Thermopylae: The Battle that Changed the World* (Woodstock and New York: Vintage and Overlook Press, 2006).

J. M. Cook, *The Persian Empire* (London: J. M. Dent, 1983).

Peter Green, *Xerxes at Salamis* (also released as *The Year of Salamis*) (New York and London: Praeger, 1970).

Charles Hignett, *Xerxes' Invasion of Greece* (Oxford: Clarendon Press, 1963).

Barry Strauss, *The Battle of Salamis: The Naval Encounter that Saved Greece – and Western Civilization* (New York and London: Simon and Schuster, 2004).

General background on Greek civilization

Paul Cartledge, *The Spartans: The World of the Warrior-Heroes of Ancient Greece, from Utopia to Crisis and Collapse* (Woodstock, New York: Overlook Press, 2003).

Robert Drews, *The Greek Accounts of Eastern History* (Cambridge, MA: Harvard University Press, 1973).

Victor Ehrenberg, *From Solon to Socrates: Greek History and Civilization during the Sixth and Fifth Centuries BC*, 2nd edn. (London and New York: Routledge, 2004).

Christopher Gill and T. P. Wiseman (eds.), *Lies and Fiction in the Ancient World* (Exeter: University of Exeter Press, 1993).

G. E. R. Lloyd, *The Ambitions of Curiosity: Understanding the World in Ancient Greece and China* (Cambridge: Cambridge University Press, 2002).

Sarah Pomeroy, Stanley Burstein, Walter Donlan, and Jennifer Roberts, *Ancient Greece: A Political, Social, and Cultural History*, 2nd edn. (New York: Oxford University Press, 2008).

James Romm, *The Edges of the Earth in Ancient Thought* (Princeton, NJ: Princeton University Press, 1994).

Other recommended reading

Ryszard Kapuściński, *Travels with Herodotus* (New York: Alfred Knopf, 2007).

Justin Marozzi, *The Way of Herodotus: Travels with the Man Who Invented History* (New York: Da Capo, 2008).

Michael Ondaatje, *The English Patient: A Novel* (Toronto: McClelland and Stewart, 1992).

Chronology

Index

Herodotus

Index

Expand your collection of
VERY SHORT INTRODUCTIONS

CLASSICS
A Very Short Introduction
Mary Beard and John Henderson

This Very Short Introduction to Classics links a haunting temple on a lonely mountainside to the glory of ancient Greece and the grandeur of Rome, and to Classics within modern culture – from Jefferson and Byron to Asterix and Ben-Hur.

'The authors show us that Classics is a "modern" and sexy subject. They succeed brilliantly in this regard … nobody could fail to be informed and entertained – and the accent of the book is provocative and stimulating.'

John Godwin, *Times Literary Supplement*

'Statues and slavery, temples and tragedies, museum, marbles, and mythology – this provocative guide to the Classics demystifies its varied subject-matter while seducing the reader with the obvious enthusiasm and pleasure which mark its writing.'

Edith Hall